RELIGIOUS VALUES IN EDUCATION

RELIGIOUS VALUES IN EDUCATION

JOHN A. STOOPS
Dean, School of Education
Lehigh University

THE INTERSTATE
Printers & Publishers, Inc.
Danville, Illinois 61832

EDITOR'S PREFACE

It is always refreshing to find something new—in format or content or both—coming from the press. Such a book is *Religious Values in Education*. In this book, which has a unique style and format, Dean Stoops deals with a timely subject in an interesting manner.

This analysis of religious values in modern education, while it may be controversial, is bound to be thought-provoking. No one interested in the philosophical basis of education can afford to ignore this book.

This work is intended to be used as a supplementary reference for teachers and prospective teachers interested in the development of a guiding philosophy of education. It should also prove of interest and value to all laymen and clergy who are deeply concerned with the religious development of American youth. Because of the wide range of interests of potential readers, the author's treatment is didactical, in part. It attempts to establish certain points of view on a vital and significant matter. Again, because of the broad gamut of interest of readers, the author has adopted a unique style of dramatizing or highlighting the issues. All major points are made in normal discourse and are reiterated, for the purpose of emphasis, in dialogue and polemic. While this manner of expression is by no means new, it has seldom been resorted to in recent educational writings.

It is well to point out that this book is presented as a work in education, not in philosophy or religion, although it should attract readers whose interests are primarily in these fields. Because the study of education is transdisciplinal, students of education draw upon and seek values in other related fields. The applications of religion and philosophy to education which the author has made are for the purposes of bringing diverse criteria to bear on the problems of education. This has been done in the hope that education will profit by these speculative outcomes, and that, thereby, teaching will be raised to a higher plane.

This book begins with the Prologue called "The Parable of the Philosophic Hen." This is followed by seven chapters. Each chapter has three parts: (1) Dialogue, (2) Polemic, and (3) Discourse. It concludes with the Epilogue entitled "A Meditation on the Romance with Social Science." Each part is explained briefly in the Introduction.

LEE O. GARBER

AUTHOR'S PREFACE

This treatise attempts an analysis of religious value in modern education. The analysis is in the existentialist mode. As such it admits of all the ontological presuppositions implicit in a belief in the primacy of man's existence and its dominance in regard to the determination of his essence. The work is intended as a supplementary reference for teachers who may be engaged in graduate study in the philosophical foundations of education. However, it has also attracted the interest of certain laymen and clergy who are deeply concerned with the religious development of American youth. Because of these several interests, the book is in part didactical, but at the same time it attempts to establish certain points of view on a vital and pressing concern of all who are interested in education.

It is necessary to point out that this book is presented as a work in education and not in philosophy or religion. Because the study of education is transdisciplinal, students of education constantly apply certain of the techniques developed in other fields to educational concerns. The applications of religion and philosophy which have been made in this study are for the purpose of bringing metacriteria to bear on the problems of religious education. This was done in hope that the speculative outcomes of these applications will contribute to leading education to higher ground in this field.

In deference to the wide range of interests this book attempts to satisfy, certain features were added to dramatize or highlight the issues. All major points are in normal discourse, but they are also presented in verse, dialogue, and polemic. These latter three forms of expression have been long used in educational writing, but they seldom appear today. (Polemic often appears today, but it is seldom labeled as such by the author.) The book begins with a Prologue called "The Parable of the Philosophical Hen." This is followed by seven chapters. Each chapter has three parts: (1) Dialogue, (2) Polemic, and (3) Discourse. The book concludes with an Epilogue called "A Meditation on the Romance with Social Science." The Prologue, the seven chapters, and the Epilogue are explained briefly in the Introduction.

In the preparation of any work the writer feels many moments of inadequacy. Probably the greatest is that moment when he attempts to record his appreciation of those who have been of assistance. The eye of his mind scans the years back to his schoolboy days, resting first upon one memory and then upon another, recalling acquaintances, some not seen in a great while, others deceased. There can be no question that over those years many words were spoken to him which gave wing to some of the thoughts which have been settled into the pages of his manuscript. An author cannot acknowledge this in any way except by expressing appreciation to all who have befriended him in the past.

The present is easier. Much of the encouragement to complete this brief work came from Lee O. Garber, Professor of Education at the University of Pennsylvania. His urgings were joined by those of Professor Merle Tate of Lehigh. Roy Eckardt, Head of the Department of Religion; Ross Yates, Dean of the College of Arts and Science; and Glenn J. Christensen, Provost of Lehigh, gave valuable help, the former two by discussing some of the issues and the latter by his comments on the manuscript. Mrs. Alice Rinehart gave valuable technical assistance in the preparation of the manuscript, and Mrs. Mary Barch provided the substantial boost which can come only from a first-rate typist with an eye for a misspelled word or broken sentence. It must be said that all of these at one time or another expressed disagreement with some of the sentiments the author expressed in this book. However, so great is their magnanimity, that none of them urged a change of substance.

The author is also impelled to express his gratitude to his parents, Charles and Ella Mae Stoops, whose careers in public education were inspiration for his own. In addition, the forbearance of his children, uneven as it was, made the hours possible for this work to be concluded; and finally, acknowledgment is due the steadfast support of Mrs. Stoops whose intense interest in this subject matter resulted in many penetrating and helpful questions, some of which, alas, have no answers in this world.

J. A. S.

TABLE OF CONTENTS

INTRODUCTION

Saint Augustine was the first great philosophic voice of the Christian clergy. In the year 410 A.D. the City of Rome was sacked by the Goths. By this event the fall of the Roman Empire was manifest, and the pagans blamed the Christians for the ruin of the city. Did Christianity not call for forgiveness of enemies and the renouncement of the world? And did it not turn citizens away from defense of the state? In 413 A.D. Augustine wrote his reply to this criticism in a powerful essay he called *The City of God*. He pointed out, in effect, that cities of the world are ever destined to perish. The citizens of the cities of the world place love of self above the love of God. Cities of such men cannot long survive. In Augustine's vision the two Cities are at absolute odds. All men must become citizens of the Eternal City of God. Their being as citizens of the temporal cities of the world flows into each of them from the higher source, the City of God.

This doctrine has not been without resounding political implications in the history of Western nations. The Medieval Church stood as a symbol of the City of God. Secular government did much of the church's work in suppressing crime and preserving order, but authority came from the divine. The Renaissance struggles of secular government against this authority are well known. But the break which set the Cities of the World apart may have occurred in the writing of the first amendment of the United States Constitution. Government was no longer subservient to the City of God. Moreover, the omnipresence of the nationalistic spirit has ordained that the religious organizations, bereft of secular authority, must become only one among the many kinds of institutions in the cities of the modern world.

In all of this, one central factor has been obscured. This obscurity is due in part to the fact that Augustine, whose doctrines unified religion and philosophy, also fashioned and fostered the idea that man can only be religious through a relationship with God. Abelard, Luther, and many others along the way found reason to differ. Luther once indicated a man's religion is that upon which "he sets his heart." Nevertheless, the view persists that those who are not in the tradition of the City of God are somehow not religious. In the simplest of ways, "The Parable of the Philosophic Hen" which appears as Prologue to this book attempts to show that all meaning extends from some kind of belief. This belief may be in God, but it could be in something else. Whatever a man's belief is, it is his way of being religious. Essentially, therefore, there cannot be a non-religious man. Thus, obscurity has created confusion.

The confusion boggles and pinches the work of education in the very important field of values. Schools are finding it very difficult to present traditional theistic vision in any significant way. The requirements brought on by legal separation of church and state have made it necessary for schools to pretend that religiousness is not fostered in any way by the educational program. The pretense is easily made because most school practitioners are unaware that the curriculum is pervaded by religious material. So persevering is the Augustinian vision that the extensive religious content of the typical school program goes unrecognized as such.

Occasionally this view is dismissed as simply another definition of religion. However, one can not defeat the argument by refusing to accept this wider definition of religion. Such a denial would be an invocation of the ancient nominalist creed that when a word is made, its concept has an independent reality. If the words "religion," "church," and "God" had no existence at all, our children would still be forming some kinds of belief upon which to build their lives. To say some of these beliefs, whatever they are, are not religious is simply to diminish the word "religious" and send us in search of another. However, this author has not found the search necessary. There is an abundance of support for this wider definition of religion in modern discourse on religion and education.

The first chapter, "Ubiquity of Choice," explains an existentialist view of the nature of man. It deals sparingly with the kinds of knowledge of which he is capable. The Dialogue and Polemic call special attention to the excessive faith in social science as a panacea for the human predicament. This is a dangerous attitude for society to hold; it is also unfortunate for those parts of the academic profession devoted to the social sciences. They are destined for a very severe public lashing when the realization grows that social sciences have not the power to "make gold out of lead."

The second chapter, "From Doubt to Syntax in Value," points out how any value syntax is dependent upon a God-idea or some kind of

God-head. The chapter delineates much of the confusion inherent in conversation about religion. In some way every man is religious. A non-religious man is either insane or impossible. Finally, it describes the irony inherent in the church-state separation and recent court decisions which have resulted in an educational *milieu* which includes virtually every God-idea except those associated with traditional theism. Although no brief is held for theism over any other God-idea, the point is that denial of this vision is inherently immoral in a society which wishes to give men complete freedom to develop their own individual religious natures.

The third chapter, "Science and the Assumption of Hierarchy," is a study of the influence of science upon one of Western man's traditional religious assumptions. In effect, even though our scientific culture is still in its early stages, it is clear that it has not challenged the assumption of hierarchy. In fact, it seems obvious that science, at this stage at least, has not only accepted it but uses it. To some scientists, science has become the basic thing in their religious nature. But even those scientists do not, in their values, question the validity of hierarchy.

The fourth and fifth chapters treat of the religious presuppositions of pantheists and atheists. Both chapters discuss the ways in which pantheism, panentheism, and atheism appear in the public school curriculum. Although these God-ideas are not framed as doctrines and presented as such, they are constant and potent influences. Perhaps their potency is even greater because their doctrinal nature is not identified and they are, therefore, truly pervasive of the school environment, not subject to the critical analysis which is brought to bear upon any doctrine soon after it appears. Here again is irony! Plato's school in the Grove of Academe was openly religious, and all academic organizations since Plato's academy have been pervaded by religious attitudes and values. But owing to the passion for separation, the modern style for academic institutions is to disclaim religiousness. This betrays either alarming ignorance or shameful hypocrisy; neither of these is flattering to the modern academic profession in America which is disposed to make much of both its astuteness and integrity.

Chapter VI, "Prayer in Religious Education," deals with the dilemma of Christian education. Christianity is not an "academic" religion. Its founders are beyond the reach of history. Christianity is highly dependent on the inward building of ideals. Thus, symbol, personification, prayer, and ritual are quite vital. An academic Christian is possible, but one does not arrive at his Christianity by the academic route. Christians must explore new ways to develop Christianity in people. It is too much, of course, to suggest that the public schools can take this on, but the public schools can either be used to help, or, if it is not possible to help, they can at least cease from obstructing the development of Christian natures.

Certain legal and administrative reforms are needed. Prayer is a way of worship, but perhaps even more importantly, it is a way of learning. Non-Christians may not easily understand this, but non-Christians certainly should understand the blessings of tolerance. Having appreciated them in their absence, they can be expected to be in the forefront of wanting tolerance as a universal condition, even the tolerance of Christianity.

The speculation called "Brave New Schools" is simply an expression of faith in the creative spirit of the American people. We must try to understand that some problems cannot be solved at the state and national level. More than this, we must try to understand that state and national involvement can only bring certain problems to new levels of desperation. The greatest contribution our states and nation can make to their solutions is to institute the legal and administrative reforms needed to allow local communities to operate as they should. Educational leaders have been prone to dismiss this "mystique of localism" and much of what they say about deficiencies in local control may be true. State and national goals need to be articulated in policy. But the thrust of the past four decades has been in the direction of less local freedom. Local freedom has been virtually "washed out" in some states. The result is that some of the problems which *only* the local community can solve are going unsolved. This matter of religious values is a case in point.

The final chapter, "The Examined Life and the Crisis in Values," reveals the author's bias toward the pre-eminence of ideals in a meaningful life. It is also a critique of certain forces in modern public education which are so devoted to skills and cognate knowledge that they are coming very close to converting public schools into special purpose institutions. The silence of public education on value development is perhaps the most coherent and eloquent statement of purpose it has rendered in the past fifty years. While it is true that nearly every general statement on public education in the United States includes a few sentences about "morality" and "self-realization," these are vague, usually by intent. This chapter does set forth a belief that public education in the last century was not so squeamish. The general reason for the modern tendency to skirt the problem is that it is far better to strive for such unity as we can achieve about our schools than to risk a divisive dialogue about value development. There is little chance, therefore, that any large organization of professionals or laymen will do anything more than strive for neutral language which will allow the individuals to think that something is happening and that, whatever that something is, it is not particularly harmful to his interests or personal leanings.

This chapter also gives emphasis to the role of ideals in human conduct. Men are excited by ideals in two ways. One is in their realization; the other is in their corruption. Much of what present-day Americans enjoy in their leisure comes from the corruption of ideality. This must be taken as symptomatic of the dissipation of civilizing influences. Only through education in ideality is there hope that these tides can be reversed.

The Epilogue, "A Meditation on the Romance with Social Science," is a polemic inspired by the recent tendency of many in school, government, and university to behave as if the social sciences could deal operationally with problems in human values. Often social science investigations of various kinds have been launched to determine educational needs. The data such studies produce are helpful in thinking about many things including the things education might do, but it is pure hocum to suggest that such studies reveal the needs education should meet. Quality education does not meet needs; it creates needs. It galvanizes a man; it does not only fulfill him. Good education is based upon human inspiration rather than human desperation.

Social science can observe and report values, but of itself, social science cannot create or prescribe them. Despite this, teacher education programs and training programs for educational administration across the nation are so dominated by the social sciences that significant exposure to humanistic foundations of education has virtually disappeared in some colleges and departments of education. Social sciences are descriptive of value development but are not and never were intended to tell men what a man *ought* to be. It is true that a social scientist will occasionally indulge in this kind of speculation with good effect; but, in so doing, he steps outside of his scientific tradition. He is speaking then as a man.

Part of the damage this romance has done is in apparently convincing many Americans that they need not aspire as individuals to anything related to social norms. Many Americans are well on the way to believing that they are social beings, tied to prescriptions ordained in the mystique of social science. It is ending, and these words are intended to encourage this ending. Soon we will learn what can be asked of social science and what can not. Soon we will restore value problems to the humane studies. This, in turn, may result in better discourse on values and also in better social science.

The Parable of the Philosophic Hen

The hens in the hen house were discontent. From their nests each day the eggs were taken, to what end they knew not. One of their number, known for the quality of her philosophic thought, was asked by all the others to meditate on the meaninglessness and absurdity of it all. Getting nowhere, this wise one decided to ask the eggman who called upon her each day to reveal to her that which is ultimate in henliness.

"Sir," said she, "what is the purpose of my life?" This eggman, being himself a reflective sort, was pleased by the question, and the two settled in the doorway of the hen house, he sitting and she perching, as he revealed to her the metaphysics of the market place and the eternal verities of the economic system. The eggman took great care to show this hen that it was her purpose to love it all with a perfect love unmixed by the primordial urges which go into the making of eggs inside her warm and feathery body.

When it was finished, she rejoined the others, and they gathered around her clamoring to know what was ultimately real. "He actually thinks people eat those things," the hen said, and they all laughed together in the derisive way that only hens can laugh. When this laughing was over one of the young ones said, "But how will we discover the purpose of our lives, and what are we to do about all this meaninglessness and absurdity?"

The philosophic hen replied: "We can only go on thinking in the way that hens can think. We must each choose something in which to believe and having chosen this we must spend our lives trying to understand it." So from that time on each hen found contentment in her own way, and the eggman knew nothing of all this because each day the eggs were in the nest at the usual time.

CHAPTER I

Ubiquity of Choice

Let not dissent bring out despair
  Or anger in your voice
A man's life is his own affair
  There's agony in his choice
Each one must face alone
  The maker of his race
If the City of God is not his home
  He chose another place.

DIALOGUE

Student: Are not men like sheep? See how they flock together, how they imitate and follow. Their lives merge as the waters of a stream; they look about and struggle to be part of the stream. Their women abide in fashion and style and they teach their young that in the flock is wisdom and goodness.

Teacher: But men are not in one flock; are there not many flocks?

Student: Yes.

Teacher: And must not a man then decide if he will join one or another of the flocks or if he will remain alone?

Student: Yes, but those who stand alone are often called mad.

Teacher: Will you agree that a man must choose from among the flocks he may join and that if he stands alone that, too, is a choice?

Student: I will.

Teacher: Then a man who chooses is not mad, but simply a man who chooses.

Student: Yes.

Teacher: Then is it correct to say that a man who chooses to stand apart is not mad, but one who is beginning a new flock or is a flock unto himself?

Student: How can that be?

Teacher: You have agreed that a man can choose?

Student: I have.

Teacher: You notice that in moments of danger brave men do brave things and other men do nothing. In moments of opportunity ambitious men vent ambition while other men stand aside. When passions are aroused some act, some speak, and others suppress themselves.

Student: That is true.

Teacher: We do not then expect the same things of all men?

Student: No.

7

Teacher: Even of men who are in a flock?

Student: No, but men who gather together are apt to be similar.

Teacher: But not alike?

Student: No.

Teacher: Very good. Can we not think that they have chosen to gather with those similar to themselves?

Student: We can.

Teacher: Presumably this joining gives comfort or contentment in some measure?

Student: Presumably.

Teacher: Then is not a man who stands apart, who is content to exist alone with his differences, and who does not require the comfort of those similar to him as a flock unto himself?

Student: I see what you mean. It is true that some men are not sheeply in nature. But most men are as sheep because they choose to flock and value as a flock.

Teacher: Does a sheep choose or not choose to join a flock?

Student: The sheep does not choose but joins the flock because it is his nature to join.

Teacher: Then a sheep has no choice?

Student: No.

Teacher: But men join because they choose?

Student: Yes.

Teacher: A sheep joins his flock because it is his nature, but a man joins because he prefers association to standing alone?

Student: That is true.

Teacher: Then a man is not as a sheep nor is his nature sheeply. Why is this so?

Student: Because he examines alternatives and must choose.

Teacher: Then if he chooses to live as a sheep is he less a man than if he chooses to live alone?

Student: No, because it is the reality of choice which makes him a man and not a sheep.

Teacher: I think you have discovered something important.

POLEMIC

What a malignancy is this social science! How degrading that our torments and passions are plated over by tissues of objectivity! Is it vanity to want to be a man? Why do we put out the eyes which turn inward to want, warmth, and beauty? Can we bear another century of this? Process. Is life no more than process? Shall we scrutinize process and thereby know life? Social science invents a man and then studies him. Very good. But am I that man? I choose not to believe this.

Society imitates its science. It invents a retirement age and informs all who pass it they are retired. It invents deprived children then informs all such children of their deprivation. It invents all kinds of men and children and searches out those to become that which has been invented. How arrogant it was for women to choose not to remain voteless! How impertinent was the Negroes' choice not to remain segregated. How tiresome it is that men will not choose to stay in their boxes. How tiresome and how magnificent it is.

The reality which underlies all human experience is the reality of choice. Man cannot avoid choosing. In the course of his life, he must constantly choose. Choices range in their nature from primordial to intellectual. Primordial choices are those of man, the creature. He loves, he eats, he seeks comfort, and he guards against danger. These deeds require decisions and the decisions are keyed to the sovereign urge in life, the urge that life shall continue and shall last.

If the human body could be thought capable of holding a belief, it would then be proper to say that the body believes in being alive. Its automatic responses respond in support of that belief in life, and the signals the body sends to the conscious will in the form of appetite or discomfort are ways the living body has of transmitting this decision to live on to a higher decision-making center. It is possible that in this higher center the body could be overruled, appetite suppressed, and discomfort endured even to the point of death. Such choices are made when that higher center of decision holds a belief that over-

9

powers even the belief in life itself. Man has this power in his power of choice.

The reality of choice pervades every level of rationality and mounts to every height or abstraction. There are the choices of life work, of education, of leaders, of responsibility, and of the good. These tend to categories of choice containing literally thousands of sub-choices, some made again and again each day, each hour. Choice is the agony and the ecstasy of life. It is that which makes a man a man and not a sheep.

Some men appear more disposed to choice than others. Appearances, however, are deceiving. Many who appear seldom to choose have elected to have their choosing done by others. Such men appear sheeply in nature, but this does not change the fact that they are men and could, at any moment, cease to choose as the flock chooses and depart from the established course of their lives and become reestablished in another.

Choice includes consequences. The consequences of any human choice are embedded in that choice. The consequence of not dressing properly for inclement weather is the increased prospects for illness. The choice of dress includes that consequence. The brooding deliberations of Hamlet were dominated by the consciousness of unknown consequences, specifically, the unknown consequences of death:

> Thus conscience doth make cowards of us all;
> And thus the native hue of resolution
> Is sicklied o'er with the pale cast of thought.

But Hamlet erred in convicting himself of a failure of resolution. He resolved to accept life and its hideous problems rather than death and its unknown dreams. There was drama in both alternatives. Choice was not avoided. It was made. Hamlet chose to live and the consequences of his choice are related in the tragedy which followed.

The ubiquity of choice is not the domination of life by choice, nor is it the status of choice as the base reality of experience. A man is the sum of his choices. So long as he has choices remaining in his life he is incomplete or unfinished. Only the past of his nature can be objectified. His last choice may make his life something altogether different. The wretched Sydney Carton who went beneath the falling knife in place of his fleeing countryman, Dorney, achieved a "sanctuary in their hearts, and in the hearts of their descendants generations hence." His last choice was "far better" than any he had ever made. Choice does not dominate life. Choice is life.

A society of men founded upon social science can be salutory if it is dominated by men who quest for humane purpose in life. But if science detours men from examination of life purpose it becomes a viper in his bosom, doubly venomous because it brings to men greater power at the same time that their contemplation of values fades and fags. It is well that processes can be examined, but processes are neither right-headed nor wrong-headed; they are simply no-headed. Only men can examine purpose. Science can not legislate the terms of man's life. The things which matter deeply are not confronted by science. Such things are left to man, the lonely individual who must choose them.

Oh, but is he not a citizen of the City of God? What of the Augustinian vision? Men who belong to God, whose souls are linked to the eternal train, do not these men serve God's purpose? Indeed they do. But their acceptance and servitude comes out of choice! They choose to be of God! More than this, they choose the idea of God which serves their passion. No, a man is not a citizen of the City of God. Each man is a city unto himself.

A city unto himself? Whatever can this mean? Each man builds for himself a city of life. He builds it out of ideals, desires, values, skills, and passions. Each man is a city; no two are alike. Each city of man is an accumulation of choices made and choices held to.

But what of God? A man's idea of God rests in the base of his city. It gives support and inclination to all that stands above. It is the foundation of the city. Change the foundation and change all else. But how shall one gain an idea of God if education conceals part of his light! Alas, here is our problem. Woe to the unborn who must choose their God without the light of traditional vision to guide them. What kind of a city can each man build? Will it be a city of processes with an ethic of success? What else will a man of today choose?

A man makes many choices but the greatest he makes is the choice of his God. This choice in some way is involved in every other choice he makes. Does a man choose his God once and never again? No. His God is chosen again and again with each conscious choice of his waking life. Those of consistent choice have a firm foundation for their personal city of man. Those of inconsistent choice live in a personal city of confusion and despair. Woe to the generations unborn if we give them not the stuff of which a firm base can be made.

DISCOURSE

Questioning and Knowing

In the current style of American education, it is possible that one could enter at the kindergarten and continue through to graduate school without encountering an experience which really matters in his life at a deep level. It is true that a student acquires skills, makes progress in certain knowledge systems, and even develops a specialty. However, the important things that shape his being more often occur outside of the classroom or, if they occur in the classroom, they are incidental to the established program. American education reflects keen interest in what students can do, but does not concern itself with what they are becoming as men. Perhaps some believe that contemplation of greatness in people is alien to the democratic spirit. However, we can not for long think that democracy and greatness are antithetical. History will shout us down.

We are closer to the problem when we consider the "answer orientedness" of the American classroom. Children bring questions to life, and they bring questions to school. Somehow the notion has grown in us that a school is a place where answers are learned. This is unfortunate for two reasons. The first is that the school does not have answers to the important questions of life. If teachers would reflect more than they do upon man's futile pursuit of cosmic ultimates, they would insist that the pose of certitude be changed. The second is that the most important things about life *are* questions. A child should not be deprived of his question. He should be persuaded to explore it further and, in the course of his education, should find his own way of coming to terms with it. This is one way of saying that the school does not answer the central questions of life. It provides an environment in which an individual conducts his own search for answers.

The question raised in the foregoing Dialogue and Polemic on whether men are as sheep is quite central to this issue. Men have questions; they must not be dominated by their gregariousness.

12

The search for wisdom on the central concerns of life is a lonely undertaking. It can only be rewarded on a personal scale. In this regard the terms "curriculum" and "course" almost become anathema when considered in the light of their etymological origins, channel, or route. There is a channel or route which shows where a man has been in his education in the central concerns of life, but there are no such things ahead which he can follow; there are only questions.

Modes of Knowing

The words "teaching" and "learning" are often linked. This linkage looks toward psychological views of education. When one links the words "teaching" and "knowing" he is moving in the direction of a view of education conventionally called philosophical. It is quite evident that the study of education in recent years has been dominated by a psychological view. This view itself is not improper, but the propriety of its domination is open to serious question.

There are at least two modes of knowing.[1] For purposes of simplicity, these can be called mode one and mode two. This simplification should not be taken too much to heart because there are profound philosophical issues involved. However, mode one and mode two can serve the purposes of this essay. Mode one is "objectified" knowledge. What kind of knowledge is this? It is the knowledge that certain described events occurred on certain days, the knowledge that the earth turns constantly and orbits the sun, and the knowledge that a certified number of people live in a place called Denver. Often such knowledge goes by the word "facts." One comes to know the facts of the world! A fact becomes fact when it corresponds to the essence of a "thing in itself." We can construct tests to determine if a knower knows such facts.

Mode two of knowing is far more complicated. There is no way to measure such knowledge. Knowing the facts of American history is one thing, but knowing how it feels to be an American and how an American feels about the "facts" of his history is something else. What is one's personal orientation to the sun? Does it not rise in the East? Does the person who knows Denver like or dislike the city? Personal knowledge of a thing is subjective. But to a humane teacher,

---

[1] Van Cleve Morris, *Philosophy and the American School* (Boston: Houghton Mifflin Company, 1961), pp. 167-170.
See also:
Jean Paul Sartre, *L'Etre et le neant* (Paris: Gamilord, 1943). Trans.: *Being and Nothingness* (New York: Philosophical Library, 1956).

this mode two knowledge should be more important than mode one. Mode two is what leads to choice, and choice is life.

An example of this can be seen in the man who planted a poplar in his back yard. Two decades of his dedicated care brought it to fine maturity. He loved the tree. He loved the pattern its barren branches cast against a January sky. In all the world there was no spot better than its summer shade. One day he sold his house and moved to another part of town. Shortly thereafter he passed by the house and was chagrined to find the tree gone. The new resident was watering geraniums growing in a spot untouched by the summer sun for many years.

Both men knew the tree at mode one. They would agree to its name, shape, and location. Even further, they would agree on its exact height or on how many leaves it held on a given August morning. But one man was a poplar buff; the other a geranium buff. At the mode two level they could not have the same knowledge of that tree, those geraniums, or, for that matter, anything. It is the mode two knowledge which led to the choice one man made to eliminate the tree and to the disappointment the other felt at his having done so.

The American classroom teacher tends to assign greater importance to mode one knowledge. This, in part, may be due to the highly impressive performance of test builders who have been successful in measuring achievement of such knowledge. Mode one knowledge can add up to a powerful argument for conservation, birth control, or personal hygiene. But little is known about crossing the gap to how one feels about these things. These feelings are personal domains and can never be regarded in any other way.

In recent years taxonomies have been developed which describe various levels of knowing. The extent to which these taxonomies offer a way for empirically based research to perform in hitherto unstudied areas remains to be seen. Some have very grave doubts (this is not to imply that they are grave about doubting). There are so many ways that a man can know a poplar tree.

Freedom and Choosing

Possibly the best way to think of the relationship between the knower and mode two knowledge is to think of the knower as becoming. The world of becoming is the environment in which the individual is establishing his self-relationships with all parts of the cosmic community. These relationships are real, they hold meaning, and they are unique to each knower. It is important to understand that as the knower is becoming, all that he is coming to know is also "becoming" for him. Thus, a child plays, and in his play he perceives, he manipulates, he fondles, he breaks, he accepts, he turns away. Here he is developing self-relationships to all he encounters.[2] It is not enough to say he is developing his world. Although it is awkward, it is better to say he is becoming a world (or a city unto himself as described in the Polemic).

Each mode two knower sits, as it were, at the center of his own becoming world. It is his own; it is as rich and full of joy as is his capacity to perceive richness and to experience joy. There are as many worlds as there are knowers. Because two knowers can not be alike, neither can two worlds be alike. Activity as seen in this light is not, as many of the pragmatic traditions suggest, related to problem-solving alone. Nor is education simply the reconstruction of experience.[3] There are external goals to education. These goals are best seen in a personal, rather than in a social context. The general goal of education is to incarnate the creative potential of each individual. This goal arrives in view when the individual comes to appreciate the life of choice which stands before him.

The key to humane teaching is not only in the full recognition of mode two knowledge but in establishing the environment of freedom essential for this knowledge to reach higher levels of power. There are many ways that freedom of self can be denied or circumscribed. One of these is to label a child. Our educational system, its teachers, and indeed the children who are in it have a predisposition to label. A label is a constrictive thing to a child. It implies limits to his becoming. Only in an elementary school classroom which is ungraded and which does not contain within it classifications of any kind, can escape the charge of labeling. Even in such a classroom the pedagogical style of the teacher can be such as to force children to accept limits to their becoming. This does not mean an environment which contains no social order or in which the will is not disciplined. It does mean the teacher preserves the freedom for self-esteem to de-

---

[2] George F. Kneller, *Introduction to the Philosophy of Education* (New York: John Wiley & Sons, 1964), p. 68.

[3] John Dewey, *Democracy and Education* (New York: The Macmillan Company, 1916), pp. 89-90.

The assertion that education is not just reconstruction of experience indicates the existentialist dissatisfaction with a popular tendency to use Dewey's "technical definition of education" as a plenary definition of education.

velop and intervenes when the children deport themselves in a manner which places strictures upon that freedom for their classmates.

This kind of classroom teacher wants children to become all they can become. His orientation is to what a child can be rather than upon what he can not be. He builds the child's development upon what the child can do and likes to do rather than on what the child finds difficult and dislikes. His teaching arts are focused upon the child as an emerging world.[4] His purpose is to produce for that world more ample possibilities for being. For such a teacher the oftcited goal of self-realization is not an empty professional charade. It is the core of his work.

Social Desperation or Human Inspiration

Americans tend to give society a kind of creature reality in which it is supposed that society has a kind of metabolism with parts which occasionally malfunction. There is much talk of social needs. The parlance of social diagnosis includes such words as "unemployment," "ghetto," and "crime rate." In recent years the approach to improving the human condition is through a "great society." By healing the raw and bleeding parts of our social system, by having the system in functioning order, the conditions necessary for human greatness will presumably emerge.

This reasoning views individual man as a social-vocal phenomena.[5] Society is the "hot house" in which he grows and flourishes. He is a "hot house plant" and works out his existence in a cultivated environment. Thus, the thrust of our educational efforts is social improvement and not man improvement, except in the sense that the latter is achieved by the former. This can add up to an appealing argument until men notice (as Americans are beginning to do) that in building such an adjusted society they are oppressed by regulation and restriction. Americans have fashioned their own chains. The "hot house" is increasingly vital to their lives. A man must not break out; all must be encompassed. The adjustments go on, and oppression grows with each turn of the screw.

This is not to imply that social action is not without effect. On

---

[4] Kneller, *op. cit.*, pp. 58-70.

[5] The term *social-vocal phenomena* has been used as descriptive of man's reality in the ontology of pragmatism. It implies that man takes his existence from the society of which he is part. The view appears consistent in Hegel's idealism which seems to have this in common with American pragmatism.

the contrary, it makes men increasingly interdependent. It makes them sheeply in nature. Neither is this to imply that social action should be avoided. The point of social action should be the *improvement of men*. For example, social security should not increase as men improve. The purpose of such social action should be to make such social action unneeded. Social security, therefore, should decrease as men improve. In a society of responsible men it should not be needed at all. Education needs vision of a society where man is made strong enough to stand forth in the elements of his world rather than to vegetate luxuriously in the comfort of his social "hot house."

Education and teaching, therefore, should center upon human inspiration and not social desperation. It is of extreme importance that each teacher look upon each child not as a social problem but as a human potential. A child is not a will that must be dominated; a child is a world that is developing. Teaching should be humane; it should bring the child into confrontation with the greatness in mankind. There is much that can be used to do this, but it all begins with a view of the school, of the child, and of mankind that has not yet been incarnated in American education.

A meaningful life is not possible without full freedom for self-realization. One who is led in his education to accept society's realization of him and to accept society's domination of him can find no meaning for his life unless he becomes a fully integrated social man. Suppose, for example, a man is made conscious from childhood onward that he is a slave, owned by others. There are places he can go and cannot go. There are things he can say and not say, do and not do, and so on. If he does not rise above this as a man, if he accepts it fully, then his life is apt to remain free of confusion. All meaning for him comes of his unquestioning obedience to the identity which is prescribed. The example is a dramatic one, seldom found in the concourse of modern life; it is chosen to illustrate a point. The well educated slave is not confused. His life has a meaning.

On the other hand, if we attempt to tell children to become what they can become, if we hold this out as an ideal, and give this sentiment a place of great honor in our documents of state, but do not fully incarnate it in the development of children we have opened their lives to meaninglessness and discontent. Society values children in school. In fact, society is extremely eloquent about what it likes and does not like about children in classrooms. The voice is expressed in the literature the children read; in the rewards the school gives out; and, above all else, in the administrative categories the school establishes for the organization and management of the curriculum.

We cannot have it both ways; either we believe in freedom and respect the potential for manhood that each individual represents or we acknowledge that he must seek meaning through his environment with social processes alone. Because a man is a man and is not a sheep we know that social meaning is, at best, contingent meaning. It is contingent on what the "mind of society"[6] believes to be good to have or of worth at any time. If a man is not (and what man is?) totally adaptive to society's valuing, the meaninglessness and absurdity of his existence in the social order will constantly oppress him. It is better then to be wholly a slave than to be half free.

Society will serve man best if it sets the conditions for his greatness. This, of course, presupposes that a free man tends towards greatness. There is much to support such a theme, and a goodly portion of that which follows is devoted to marshalling it for the reader's view. Thus, the first duty of a society is to set the conditions of man's freedom, and to assure that the widest possible array of alternatives are presented for the exercise of his choice.

------

[6] Donald Butler, *Four Philosophies and Their Practice in Religion and Education* (New York: Harper and Brothers, 1951), pp. 453-456.

CHAPTER II

From Doubt to Syntax in Values

Manner and pride are oft arrayed
  To form a man's facade.
But movement is a mere charade
  Without a choice of god.
Choose the mundane and live the years
  In the dread of mortality
Or choose ideals and quiet the fears
  In devotionality.

DIALOGUE

Student: Men are not so religious as once they were. Often they
           mock their priests or rabbis. The great judges have or-
           dered that ceremonies of the Holy Book cease and they
           have forbidden that children worship in the public schools.
           Some are saying that God is dead, and what once they
           called His providence or wrath are now but the inexorable
           ways of nature.
Teacher: These things have happened, but have you noticed that men
           still call upon one another to do good things and to stop
           doing bad things? Is it not true that men still desire or
           value the good?
Student: Yes, I think they do.
Teacher: Then men are still inclined to make distinctions between
           bad and good?
Student: They are.
Teacher: Each man has a basis for choosing what is good for him
           or bad for him; he also has a basis for knowing what he
           likes or likes not?
Student: He has.
Teacher: Do you also agree that some men still accept the revealed
           word of God of our Holy Scripture as a base for knowing
           what is good or not good or what to like or not like?
Student: It is true that some men accept the revealed words of God
           as a base for the good. But what of those who do not?
Teacher: I see. We think of these Godly men as religious. But we
           call those who look elsewhere for values as not religious?
Student: Yes.
Teacher: Let us see if this is true. We have agreed that men base
           values elsewhere than in gods and are still concerned with
           what is good and with what they prefer and so forth?
Student: We have.
Teacher: So all men value.

21

Student: They do.

Teacher: Some get their values through an idea of God as revealed
            to them in scripture and church tradition and, because we
            have also agreed that men choose, can we now accept
            that men who have this traditional God-idea have chosen it
            in preference to others?

Student: What others?

Teacher: We will deal with this later. Can we now agree that he
            has chosen to believe what he believes?

Student: We can.

Teacher: Can we then say that his choice of this traditional idea
            is his way of being religious?

Teacher: Of course.

Student: And a base for his hierarchy of values?

Teacher: Yes.

Student: This God-idea is often called traditional theism. Will you
            concede that men can have other God-ideas such as pan-
            theism or atheism?

Student: How can atheism be a God-idea?

Teacher: Is not any idea of God a God-idea?

Student: Of course.

Teacher: Is not an idea that there is no God as much a God-idea
            as an idea that there is a God?

Student: I suppose so.

Teacher: Well, if your supposition is true, is not an atheist religious
            in a different way from a theist? And can not he be as
            devout in whatever way that is? And does he base his
            values on whatever he places in the place the theist places
            God?

Student: I see what you mean. An atheist must choose something to
            take the place of God.

Teacher: And this becomes his God-idea.

Student: Of course.

Teacher: And his way of being religious?

Student: Yes.

Teacher: Can you imagine a value holding man without some kind
            of God-idea?

Student: No.

Teacher: And we have agreed that all men hold values?

Student: All men do.

Teacher: Then do you know of any man whom you cannot call religious?
Student: There is no man of whom I can say, "He is not religious."
Teacher: You have discovered something else worth knowing.

POLEMIC

Renaissance! New birth! The Fourteenth Century was lighted by new fires. They flared for three hundred years. Descartes, Bacon, Spinoza, and Locke were sons of an epoch which generated new men of self-conscious freedom. But the fires burned brightest in men who were alive to discovery. They discovered the world in voyages at sea. They rediscovered man in voyages to pagan and Biblical antiquity. Men came to know the wealth of their minds, the value of their speculations, and the importance of their lives. They authored a new spirit which moves today in the modern world.

The sons of the Renaissance built bridges to modern philosophy. Of all the great expressions which link modern men to this precursory generation, none seem more attuned to the modern spirit than Descartes' adventure in doubt. In developing foundations for what was to become a philosophy of science he began by doubting everything except his own existence. After breathing deeply of the galvanic atmosphere of his times, Descartes was prepared to begin by doubting all. He then searched for a single certainty upon which to build his philosophy. This certainty he found to be his own existence. This he refused to doubt because "I am; I exist; how often? As often as I think."[1] By way of further explanation Descartes declared: "What is it that I am? A thinking thing. What is a thinking thing? It is a thing that doubts, affirms, denies, wills, abstains from willing, that also can be aware of images and sensations."[2]

What heroism this is! The incomparable Descartes! Raised up by Jesuits,[3] tested as a soldier, he developed a philosophical method out of a belief in nothing but the massive fact of his own existence.

---

[1] René Descartes, *Meditations on First Philosophy* (1641). Trans.: Norman Kemp Smith, *Descartes: Philosophical Writings* (New York: Modern Library, 1958).

[2] *Ibid.*

[3] T. V. Smith and Marjorie Crene, eds., *Philosophers Speak for Themselves: From Descartes to Locke* (Chicago: University of Chicago Press, 1940), p. 12.

What did his existence mean? It restored Aristotle to science; it made Newton possible; it gave method to the ideal of a rational science. This existence was no small thing. Descartes and his co-revolutionists remade the Western mind. How was this done? They made doubt an honorable thing to own!

It is a short way from the philosophy of doubt to the philosophy of choice and from this to a philosophy of values, that literature of the inner man which has dazzled the European mind in the last one hundred fifty years. We cannot deny that existence requires choice and choice requires valuing. How are values acquired? How are values arranged that they bear upon choices to be made? Those who teach the becoming man in his two short semesters of childhood and adolescence are well advised to ponder these questions!

William James[4] wrote of a lady whom he encountered in a discussion of cosmic reality who asserted to him that the world rested upon a rock. When concern was expressed to her about this she responded by saying this rock rested upon another rock. Further plied with questions she proclaimed: "It's rocks all the way down." The metaphysics of values are as perplexing to philosophers as the physics of the cosmos are to the lady who fixed our world atop a bouyant pile of rocks. Do values rest upon something or do they float free and undocked? Surely they rest upon something.

If values are unanchored and unpatterned they would be present at one time, not present another time, or in the constant turbulence of rearrangement. If a man's values are characterized by any of these conditions, his choices would be unpredictable. But are a man's choices unpredictable? No. Most choices a man makes can be predicted by any who know this man. Those making these predictions will say that they "understand his inclinations," and that safe predictions are possible because the "inclination" is understood. Does this not make it reasonable to think that values are anchored to something? The presence of a meaningful inclination also makes possible the belief that values are organized into a syntax.

How can this arrangement of values be described? Is there a mathematics that will compose it for view? Will a geometer display it in triangles, circles, or squares? Or can we say they sway and sail as the tail on a kite? Men do change in their inclinations. They value one way one year and another way the next. But we must believe the

---

[4] William James, *Essays on Faith and Morals* (New York: Longman Green and Co., 1943), p. 82

value arrangement has a base and gives off degrees of consistency. The elements of a system are easily seen. How can it be described? Perhaps the best that can be done is to return to the vision of "a world on the rocks."

This man, this thinking thing who doubts, affirms, denies, wills, and abstains from willing must choose a foundation for value. *He must choose a bottom rock.* The arrangement of values which is borne by the rock and which rises above it is also chosen. The base will have a shape. Its slope or pitch will communicate a dynamic to the value system. It is steady at times, changing at times but constantly there, crisply revealing itself in his every life decision.

Shall we make a record of the choices of a man? Would scrutiny of this record reveal the nature of the bottom rock? We can assume that it would teach us something of that foundation. We could call it the deep base of the man's value system. We could say that it is his fundamental belief. But may not a man have more than one fundamental belief? And would each belief not support an arrangement of values? We cannot believe this. If many beliefs are "fundamental" then we must go further down. At the bottom there must be one.

One would expect the conscious, existing, thinking man to be fully aware of the base for certainty which he has chosen. Usually he is not, nor is he aware of the exact time he installed it in place. Was it in his cradle? During childhood? In church? In school? It must have been during these years when it was selected, adjusted, and put down. One bright and very full day in the life of the young man he experiences his existential moment, on this day it can be said, the installation is complete, and the man is choosing free.

What can we call this bottom rock? It imparts syntax to his arrangement of values. It shapes his decisions about the good. It sends him here or there in the world of people and places to do the things he does. We have assumed (although the assumption will be questioned) that it was developed intellectually or conceptually and did not arrive by a genetic route. So it can be called an idea. It grows and stands as the sovereign and ruling passion of life. It is the object of his sublime adoration. So we may use the word God. Let us then call this bottom rock his *God-idea!*

Indeed, the *God-idea* may be of the God of Judeo-Christian tradition. This tradition contains an assortment of God-ideas. The vast majority of them are of a type which men call traditional theism. On the other hand, many *God-ideas* are not of the Judeo-Christian tradition. In some men their chosen God-idea has no association with any "religious practice" which is generally recognized as a religious practice and is known by the word religious. Whether it is or is not associated with religious practice the chosen God-idea is, for each man, his way of being religious. There are many modes of religious behavior. All of these modes have their manifestation in the performance of values, the enactment of choice. Therefore, religion is everywhere! There is no man of whom it can be said, he is not religious!

There is great confusion about this, and what great anguish this confusion brings. In the parlance of law and public discussion, religious conduct is usually taken to mean the exercise of attitudes or expressions directly associated with corporate religious organizations. Many in America are religious in this way, but many, *and perhaps most*, are not. Some members of religious organizations who participate regularly in religious ceremony are religious in other ways. Going to church is not their way of being religious, although they are constantly seen in churches and take an active role in church work. For such men it appears true that their involvement in religious organizations is a matter of deference to a God that is past, is dead, or who, in any case, takes no meaningful part in the choices which constitute their lives.

Our national government is founded, on part, upon a notion of religious neutrality. In this larger meaning for religiousness, the assumption of religious neutrality becomes absurd! It merely comes to a disassociation from committed corporate religious organizations. Such disassociation does not produce religious neutrality. On the contrary, it establishes a more favorable environment for God-ideas which are based in social, political, academic, or business institutions. These institutions are as capable of producing God-ideas as are recognized religious organizations.[5] Government finds no problem in its associations with secular institutions and the religious influences of secular institutions spreads with each generation. They flourish in a garden of illusions. What are these illusions? They are illusions that men are not religious about success in business, politics, society, and personal relations. How can a nation build itself on such illusions?

Students of government have researched the thoughts of our founding fathers to discern the intention of separating church and state. It seems obvious they were not attempting to sever the God of traditional theism from corporate public life. This has been dis-

---

[5] See Chapter IV.

avowed time and again. The purpose was to remain separated from churches which teach of Him or presume to minister His word and will. The reasons for this appear to be far more practical and far less ideological than they are often represented.[6] In addition, the church is not what it was; neither is government what it was; nor is the religious nature of the people what it was. What then is the current struggle? We strive to bring all elements of the problem back to the surface for re-examination, rethinking. The crises of values in American life certainly demands no less than this, and those who teach children must be at or near the front.

---

[6] It is widely agreed that the purpose of the Constitution and Bill of Rights was to provide a basis of unity for a widely diversified people. Religion and education were, in part, excluded as a practical course of action in support of the purpose. Some early Nineteenth Century interpretations of the first amendment took the word *Congress* to mean exactly that. Later this word came to mean all forms and levels of American government.

DISCOURSE

Certainty to Doubt

Would that we might once again behold the American farm boy of a generation past. His life is worthy of contemplation. It offers an example of serenity gone by. On a quiet summer night we might witness an enchanting tableau. The boy is seated at a table in the light of an oil lamp; spread before him are the open pages of the great family Bible. His expression is solemn but earnest and alive with the fascination he feels for the vivid illustrations in his gaze. There are Eden, the man, the woman, the tree, the snake; and there are the ark, great dark clouds, the old man and his sons; and there is the fierce old prophet coming down the hill carrying in his hands the tablets of stone.

The boy holds a reverence for this book. Even its location in the home reflects the veneration and esteem in which it is held. Its first pages contain the records of family births, marriages, and deaths, each carefully inscribed as if written on the heart of truth itself. The boy can get full meaning from the stories of the patriarchs and their great herds, for, after all, his father speaks with the authority of life, and he has been witness to the birth and death of many animals. He also has sheep and cattle, and his family gives a tenth of what they have to God. His family, too, is bound up in a common enterprise in which each member is needed, wanted, and expected to do his share. All are locked together in a remarkable blending of independence and interdependence.

And on that same summer night he can walk from his house and look up to a sky spangled with billions of light points, a shimmering resplendence, the source of awe and wonder for mankind since first man could look aloft. There, in the face of infinity, this boy might gaze across the flat earth which he knows as the nourisher of the living and resting place of the dead, and the feeling grows in him that he is standing on God's earth and looking into God's heaven.

The American farm boy of a generation past was not taught of his mammalian ancestry. He heard the earth was round "like an apple," but this made no deep impression. There was cozy simplicity in his certainty that it was all in the great, good book. His parson would tell him how the words of the scriptures would govern the course of his life. The American farm boy of a generation past knew certainty. His generation was the last to receive the gift of certainty.

The American farm boy of a generation past was brought to these pages to help us see the colossal change which has been wrought. The American schoolboy of today has the gift of doubt. He is told of his mammalian history and of the great reptiles which preceded his mammalian forebears and were vanquished by them. He is informed that his species is the most advanced among the mammals which are themselves the most recent general type of creature evolution.

He is a mammal! An animal which tends to keep its own temperature rather than cool as the earth cools and warm as the earth warms. He is an animal which keeps its embryonic young in its own body rather than in eggs laid upon the ground. He is told his earth is part of a solar system which is a small component of one of many galaxies. How many? The number is infinite! "Above" and "below" are relative only to an observer and have no reality. His summer nights are lighted by the fluorescent and incandescent lamps of men. This schoolboy may never see the stars of a summer night.

For him there is no cozy certainty. He is exposed to knowledge systems which transcend his perceptions. This knowledge explains most of what he sees and leads him on to new questions. He is given standards of critical thought which make the traditional explanations of man's origin seem incredible. Shielded from nature, a social concern, his generation is the first to receive the gift of doubt.

Doubt to Confusion

Those who write of children's thought describe it as egocentric at the outset.[7] It deals with creature concerns, matters of appetite. A child wants what he wants and needs what he needs, and much of his thinking centers on how to come by his wants and provide for his needs. Some have called this thinking autistic.[8] Autistic thought

---

[7] J. Piaget, *The Moral Judgment of the Child* (New York: Harcourt, 1932).
[8] David Russell. *Children's Thinking* (Waltham, Mass.: Blaisdell Publishing Co., Copyright 1956, Ginn and Co.), p. 187.

can lead to moral aphorisms. Children become infuriated with play-
mates who move ahead of turn or fail to share. Children at play encounter the first problems of government. Although they may begin
to sense the doubt of their origin, their cogitation is dominated by
the concerns of the creature.

Such concerns taken into the context of social experience can
lead to a value system. An example of this might be Kant's moral imperatives which are derived from practical reason. Moral maxims can
be developed out of the experience of life alone. Men do not need
external authority for this. A number of the maxims which are
characteristic of the morality of Western culture are found in the
Bible. Even so, there is much good reason to suspect they evolved out
of necessity. This is particularly so of the great structure of law
developed in the first five books of the Old Testament. One could
easily suppose these laws also were moral imperatives, conceived
through practical reason, and ascribed to a deity that they may have
the status of law. This supposition would be consistent with presuppositions many social philosophers in the pragmatic tradition make
about such religious aphorisms.

However, in applications to the problems of religious education,
there is a fatal weakness in this modern social philosophy. Oddly
enough the weakness occurs in the absence of a metaphysics which,
paradoxically, is a point which social philosophers conceive as a great
strength. But is it really strength to have no metaphysics in a philosophy
which must confront the problems of the individual man? The existential man raises metaphysical questions. He raises them constantly.
He wants to form an identification with his cosmic origin and cosmic
destiny.[9] Though existential man does not contest social reality, he
does not cease his interest in what is ultimately real for him alone.
In each developing man this stands as a deep personal need or want.
As such, it is an extension of autistic thought, and is as urgent and
inevitable as any other aspect of self-concern in self-development.

At this point in his thought extension, the American farm boy
of a generation past was given certainty. There was little to challenge
this certainty, and he began valuing in terms of a belief in the Biblical
God, His authority, and His concerns. Protestants turned to their
clergy for interpretations of scripture and, in some cases, church doctrine. Catholics turned to their clergy for interpretations of church

---

[9] Morris, *op. cit.*, p. 386.

doctrine and, in some cases, scripture. Jews turned to their teachers and books for interpretations of custom, tradition, and law.

It can be demonstrated that more than occasionally the God-fearing man projects his thought into religious expression. It is by no means a simple matter for a man to objectify his creature concerns. It is very difficult to do this, and one may well suppose it is rarely done. So, in the verbal expressions of a God-fearing man, God often comes out saying what the man wants or needs. Even so, this believer in God has a framework for values. It is a kind of "grid" which he places across his world which he uses to measure or value the things which are in it. The development of this "grid" is what, in this case, we call religious education. It is the education of the believer in the effects of his beliefs.

But today the child who is ready to extend his thought to spiritual concerns does not have a cozy, ready-made certainty with which to begin.[10] He begins with doubt. However, one can not manage a coherent life on a foundation of doubt. Doubt must be replaced by possibility, by assumption, or by belief. What belief will be chosen? Will the child, for example, accept his society as this foundation? or economic success? or the ideals of a craft? Probably he will not be conscious of the choice he makes. It is more likely that he will drift into belief in one of the several patterns of pantheism, or he may begin to operate on atheistic precepts, or, on the other hand, he may accept theism.

What of those who come out of it saying they have no belief in God? Does this mean they have no belief? Assuredly, it does not. They believe something which stands in their thinking where the Biblical God stands in the thinking of Godly men. A pantheist sends Christmas cards. He might be found attending the Christian mass. He joins the P.T.A. and contributes more than his quota to the Community Chest. What has made these things something he wants or needs to do? Consciously or unconsciously he has chosen a belief to replace doubt. When matters relating to his belief come to pass, he knows his mind and makes his choice.

Why do some atheists march in peace demonstrations or protest parades? Why do they write letters to legislators and newspaper editors? Institute legal proceedings against a town council or a school

---

[10] Lawrence K. Frank, *Society as the Patient* (New Brunswick, New Jersey: Rutgers University Press, 1950). Cited by Henry Ehlers and Gordon C. Lee, *Crucial Issues in Education* (New York: Henry Holt and Co., 1960), p. 175.

board? Give money to a Catholic orphanage? Such men believe in something, too. Atheists and pantheists also have a "grid" through which they survey their respective worlds. They also use this to determine the good and bad, the right and wrong, the movements to be helped and the actions to be opposed.

All three—atheist, pantheist, and theist—have a system of values. They have acquired mode two knowledge. The theist replaces doubt with God. The pantheist replaces doubt with a social, humanistic, or materialistic version of God. The atheist uses empirical standards of knowledge, develops a rationale for nature or evolution, or uses some other presupposition. Why is only the theist religious? Why are not the other two religious as well? Why do we think of the value education of the theist as religious and the value education of the others as secular? Semantic analysis renders such distinctions absurd. Nevertheless, discourse on religious education goes on and on about this distinction as if it were not only real, but quite profound. The error has been amplified by the courts. More discourse of this kind can lead only to more error, more difficulty, and less effective religious education for all.

Confusion to Irony

The implications seem ironic. Many histories of church and state have been developed. Indeed, a considerable number have been written with particular reference to religious education. Almost without exception the first amendment, as stated, is noted with approval.[11] The prevailing tendency is to treat the church with respect but to applaud the judicial interpretations which have been forcing church out of government and its services. Only a few have noted that while the church has been forced with increasing resolve to stand aside from government-sponsored activities, these same government-sponsored activities are moving toward a larger and larger role in the development of individual lives and toward more and more domination of the institutional order. This can be made to sound sinister. It is not sinister at all. The applications of an emerging social philosophy would place individual man in a position of increasing deference to government as the major institution of society.

---

[11] A typical approbation of the separation of school and "religion" is found in: Zechariah Chaffee, Jr., *The Blessings of Liberty* (Philadelphia: J. B. Lippincott Co., 1956), pp. 265-266.

However, the corresponding resolve to keep the church out of this has both profound and ironic implications.

The irony is developed from the circumstance that Godly men established the first amendment largely in the hope that it would help assure religious freedom. Now if the public schools were indeed God-less, as some devout theists have complained, the present situation would be logically tenable and consistent with the covenant implied in the moral traditions and legal foundations of our nation. But, as we have shown, the schools are God-less only in the sense that the Biblical God is barred. Other kinds of gods are present, although the word "god" is not (and perhaps should not be) used in referring to them.

It is said, of course, that the Biblical God can be taught at other times such as Wednesday afternoons after school, Saturdays, and Sundays; however, we should recognize immediately that the prime time has gone to the competing alternatives. Moving to more neutral ground, let us propose that algebra be taught Wednesday afternoons after school, Saturday, and Sunday. If such a plan were effectuated, the complaints from mathematics specialists, academic authorities, and defense planners would destroy it before the first week was finished. It is simply not a good time to teach an important subject, and algebra would be restored to its place in the daily program.

It is also said that the Biblical God can be taught in a course "about religion." As such he would appear as a phenomenon in academic discourse. In this sense he can be presented as objectified mode one knowledge. He is a thing to be known about, but he can not be presented as something to which one becomes devoted. Teaching about God must be done in the academic style. The question must then arise: Does this help provide a religious education?

Those disposed to favor a theistic solution to the great metaphysical problems would do well to ponder with care the advisability of settling the current issue with courses "about religion." If the Biblical God is brought into school wearing academic garments he would be welcomed by pantheistic and atheistic intellectuals as a colleague but not as God. Academic treatment of God will not lead to acceptance of Him as the divine. On the contrary, there is good reason to expect it will set off an opposing tendency. Such courses are useful, interesting, and academically respectable, but they serve another purpose. They do not make men religious.

What Might be Done

What might be done? No administrative solution is possible without legal reform, neither is a curriculum solution possible without legal reform. No other kind of solution is in view. Perhaps it is wrong to think that either an administrative or curricular solution must be accepted before seeking the legal reforms necessary for it to be introduced. One thing which might be done is to proceed with the legal reforms which will make true religious freedom possible.[12] If an innovative, imaginative populace has the freedom to act, solutions to its problems begin to appear.[13] Such an approach has the beauty of being consistent with the American inclination, and those who exult in democracy and in its processes would have the satisfaction of seeing them back in action on this vital problem.

What else might be done? Even without legal reform it is possible to identify the value-forming elements of the school program and study how these elements operate in the syntax of developing values. It would be far better if each of us could discover the real religion of our lives and the developing religion in the lives of our children. This alone will not settle the issues, but it will put them in a better perspective. Any reduction of the present confusion must be counted as a gain, for men in a common enterprise will go further if all can see better what that enterprise is doing! We can put faith in the prospect that a move to higher ground will furnish the perspective needed. We can also put faith in an expectation that the better perspective will show solutions which can not be seen from where we now stand.

---

[12] Freeman R. Butts, *The American Tradition in Religion and Education* (Boston: The Beacon Press, 1950).

[13] W. W. Brickman and Stanley Lehrer, ed., *Religion, Government and Education* (New York: Society for the Advancement of Education, 1961).

CHAPTER III

Science and the Assumption of Hierarchy

Science proclaims its doubts to man
  As gift for those unborn.
Is this the surety we plan
  Ere certainties foresworn?

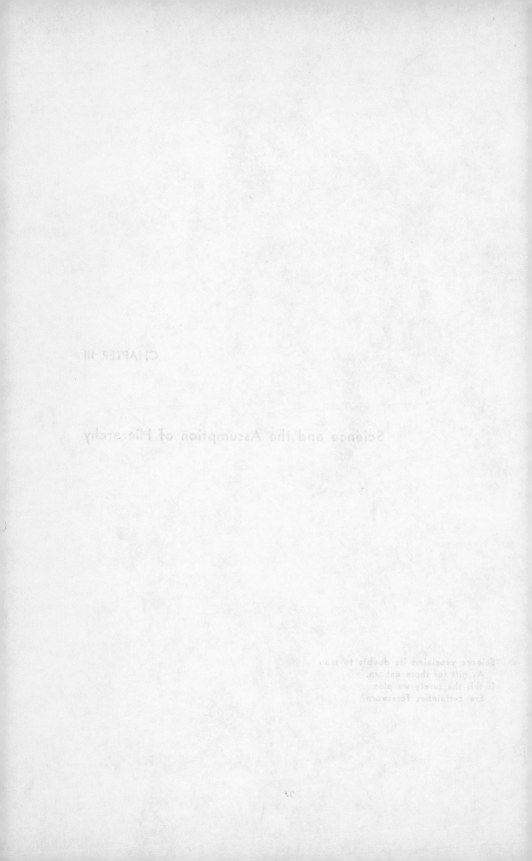

DIALOGUE

Student: In an age of men who cherish reason and science is it not possible for a God of miracles who stands with and without nature to be revered? There are causes to all events and in a science of nature all natural events have natural causes. How can a man of science or reason accept a God of supernature?

Teacher: Let us see if they can. Do you understand a meaning for the word "essence"?

Student: I want your help with that.

Teacher: We may think of essence as the quality a thing has which makes it possible for us to know it and to distinguish it from all other things, such as the treeness of a tree or the frogness of a frog.

Student: I see. Or the appleness of an apple or the grapeness of a grape?

Teacher: Very good. Now for long it has been disputed whether these qualities by which we know the world existed before the world, if they have existence in only the things themselves or if they exist only in the form of words. But that need not concern us for we can agree that these qualities we call essences have existed.

Student: You mean, for the moment, we can set aside questions of the origins of essences and concern ourselves with only their existence.

Teacher: Yes. Let us take up one metaphysical problem at a time. Now if all essences have this quality we call existence, is it proper to think that all things have this quality in the same degree?

Student: I don't understand.

Teacher: A rock exists, but it does not have what we call life; it moves very little. Centuries must pass before its changes can be perceived. Contrast this with a rose bush which has life, changes from day to day, puts out flowers, and has the capacity to produce more of its kind. Do these two things exist in the same way?

Student: No. The bush has a higher existence.

Teacher: Very good. Now what about a squirrel? Not only does it have life, but it moves about, makes a home, and guards against predatory dangers. Is not this existence higher than a bush?

Student: Yes.

Teacher: What of man, he does all this and, in addition, he develops science and reason, technology, and philosophy? Is man a higher existence than a squirrel?

Student: Yes.

Teacher: Do you suppose that if a squirrel could think, he would think that his existence was highest?

Student: Probably so.

Teacher: But he would be wrong?

Student: Yes.

Teacher: A squirrel would be as wrong as a man might be wrong to think of his existence and his perception the highest and fullest. So, is it reasonable to think that since man is higher than bushes, rocks, and squirrels in the hierarchy of being, then there are perhaps many forms of being which stand above him and which are unperceived by him as he is unperceived by a bush?

Student: Yes, that is very easy to believe.

Teacher: Even for a man of reason or science?

Student: Yes. Especially for a man of reason for this conception seems very reasonable. But what is it that stands at the top of all?

Teacher: Let us see if we can discover this. All that men see including men is endowed with existence?

Student: Yes.

Teacher: And higher forms are animated by life processes?

Student: Yes, and animation ceases when the processes cease?

Teacher: Have you noticed that a sunflower turns its face toward the sun and keeps its face fixed thereon as the day passes?

Student: Yes.

Teacher: Do you suppose the sunflower sees the sun and thinks, "There it is; I shall look at it."

Student: No.

Teacher: And when the sunflower dies, does the sun cease to make its appearance?

Student: Of course not.

Teacher: You are right; without the sun soon there would cease to be flowers of any kind. Let us apply this lesson to the idea of existence. All things turn toward pure existence. Even though there be other things higher than man, all are made animate by this quality; all are given their status by this quality; all turn toward it; all wish to be united with it. We can think of it as pure being.

Student: Then that which is called "Being" could be thought of as recreating the world by endowing its parts with the quality called existence.

Teacher: Some great philosophers and scientists seem to have thought of it this way.

Student: Such a God, if conscious of himself and of men, could very easily intervene in the business of life at any point in the hierarchy?

Teacher: Why not? If we think of God as existence itself His capacity for act would be very great.

Student: Then I was wrong to suggest that a man of reason and science could not accept a God of miracles?

Teacher: It does not seem correct to say such a general statement is right or wrong. Simply say that many eminently rational men have found an intellectual path to a supernatural God and that their science does not discourage this belief.

Student: I see.

POLEMIC

Religion is everywhere! Define a man; he is a religious problem! Why is this so? A man is born with a question; he dies with the same question. Who am I? How am I involved in this cosmic community? To this question the cosmos makes no answer.[1] Only the question echoes back to the harkening man word by word, still a question. Somewhere is there a soft message of assurance? What does existence offer? Only perception, reason, and experience. These give no truths except the truth of existence itself. After man proclaims he exists, what else can be known? He must look at what he sees and try to see more. He must consult his experience and the experience of others, especially the others who reach for religious truth. Then he must construct his beliefs. Men must have beliefs; without them, life is madness.

For 350 years men have possessed science. Science did not come to man easily or quickly. Once possessed, he has retained it only by hard work.[2] Think of the long span which encompassed man's biological development, that dimly known struggle across thousands of centuries, mutation by mutation, first up one path, then upward along another, until gradually, inexorably, the paths and adaptations become so numerous as to overcome the oppressing probabilities against such a cataclysmic event as the evolution of intelligence. Perhaps reason first faltered, but finally rationality held its ground. Think also of the thousands of centuries during which this thought-bearing creature formed culture, developed technologies, established civilizations, acquired letters, rose to the level of philosophy, faltered and finally began to hold philosophic ground. What is 350 years? Science came yesterday. We have only its first flush! This is its moment of

---

[1] Morris, *op. cit.*, p. 386.
[2] Joseph Still, *Science and Education at the Crossroads* (Washington, D. C.: Public Affairs Press, 1958), p. 61.

springtime! It is not mature; it does not know its height nor weight. To what dimensions will it grow?

Man is not scientific by nature. If science were man's nature, what kind of a nature would that be? No feeling, no emotion? Of what worth is life that has no compassion? Do not scientists become angry with other men, or with each other, or with themselves? Is it not unscientific to be ambitious? If scientific men must forsake anger and ambition, then there are but few scientific men. Perhaps there have been none since Bacon, and he reached these sublime levels only in his last days.[3]

It takes a great effort to be scientific. Few men can behave in a scientific way for very long. Suppressing passion is not eliminating passion. Suppression of anything so formidable as human passion requires a very great effort. More than this, it is only the very extraordinary scientific man who approaches more than just his scientific interest scientifically. Men of science frequently deceive themselves with an illusion that they are scientific in their attitudes toward many things. Usually scientific performance is confined to a special field of scientific interest.

But what a remarkable thing it is! How much it has taught us of the physics of a solar system! How much better we see the life processes of man and of society! How much contentment it has wrought for the creature comfort and pleasure! How it protects us from the ancient dangers of hunger and exposure! How it has added time to life and to the time needed to examine life's meanings! It is a tool. Its potency is admirable and astonishing. Men have had it only a brief interval. Look at what they have done with it!

Look indeed! The look tells us that science has given power but not discretion. Men can see better, strike harder, dig deeper, build higher, but they have not greater wisdom; they have not reached the "place of understanding."[4] What can science say of God? Science is a tool; it can say nothing of God or of anything. Science has no voice; only man has voice. If a scientist speaks of God it is a man that is speaking. His science has given him a disciplined way of looking and an agreed way of deciding knowledge, but the tool has said nothing; only the man has spoken.

---

[3] Loren Eisley, "Francis Bacon," one of a collection of articles in a volume called *The Light of the Past: A Treasury of Horizon* (New York: American Heritage Foundation, 1965), pp. 169-183.

[4] Job 28:20.

Science cannot say there is or is not a God. It cannot say what is His nature. Science can only help men examine the evidence upon which beliefs can be built. There is but one exception. Some men have found it possible to accept science itself as God. Of such men little can be said except that they appear to be worshipping an epistemology. This is not a new thing for men to do. The Pythagoreans found satisfaction in the worship of numbers, and this tendency lingers here and there in the community of men. There is a view in theology that men create whatever they worship. This is but one atheistic style of God-idea.

Science has helped men know that there is much beyond and beneath the gaze which the eye does not reveal. The eye of science has detected the particle and the gene. It has uncovered the galaxy and much that is somewhat beyond. It has given us a view of our earth in time and has shown man how to become a developing thing which was once not so great and is now greater.

But science has not destroyed *the assumption of hierarchy*. In some ways it has made it more tenable. Science tends to reinforce the ancient notion that there is an order in nature. It has produced good and distinct reasons for thinking that some things are higher than others. It has led to plausible theories as to why one species increases in number, strength, and complexity while another weakens and disappears. Science affirms that movement is on-going, never ceasing; that involution, evolution, and revolution are constant[5] and forever. All is a welter of endless transformation. Permanence and invariance are found only in certain ideas of men.[6]

Can there be cause without event, a motion without a mover? Does nature respond to laws, laws of its own making? Who is the unmoved mover? Who imparted motion to all that moves? If we find principles to which nature obeys, who impressed such principles on the matter and the motion of the world?

Science helps us to know that man stands at the top of any scale of creature complexity. So man is found to stand above his fellow creatures in the hierarchy of complexity; his power of reason alone produces an immense vertical gap between man and his nearest kin. (This is not to claim that there are not reasoning powers in animals

---

[5] Cassius J. Keyser, *The Human Worth of Rigorous Thinking* (New York: Scripta Mathematica, 1940), p. 162.

[6] One of the best known exposures of this view is in *The Meno*, a dialogue in which Plato developed his theory of knowledge.

or that men are "superior" creatures by every physical or moral standard.) However, science has produced nothing which would destroy an assumption that men see only a portion of the hierarchy. This hierarchy which science sees so clearly and which man surmounts so easily is all of the hierarchy that is visible to man in the application of his science.

But there may be much more to the hierarchy. Man may be only at its mid-point. Indeed, he may not even stand that high. We are reasonably certain that forms of being which stand below where men stand are unaware of the above-standing of men. Why is it not then reasonable to suppose that forms of being stand above men who are likewise unaware of what stands above. Moreover, men have seemed naturally disposed to assume that a higher being exists. What is the meaning of this disposition? The belief in hierarchy is consistent with the religious posture most traditional in American life. Science offers nothing which disturbs such a belief.

Does science deny God? No. Is science producing men who do not believe in God? No. Science does not promote nor does it discourage belief in God except in the cases where Science is made into a God-idea in its own right. Here the believer is placed in a difficult contradiction. Science commands objectivity by its users. One would be entitled to suppose then that the scientist would be highly objective in his view of the role of science in the affairs of men. "Science worship" on the other hand takes its form in the abandonment of this objectivity and the postulant becomes decidedly unscientific about his science.

However, a believer in hierarchy will find that science does not destroy such a belief. It is necessary to be cautious about saying this. Science does not establish hierarchy. It simply fails to demolish the assumption of hierarchy. If a scientist is devout in his acceptance of hierarchy, this devout acceptancy did not derive from his work as a scientist. He came to believe it as a man, but he found that his science raised no objection.

DISCOURSE

Science and the Nature of Man

Now that a scientific tradition has been sustained for over three centuries, it is of some urgency that we consider the long-range effects of such a tradition on the nature of man. Speculation on this has been usually confined to the new technologies and the comfort, safety, convenience, and material abundance now at man's disposal. But reference here is not to such externals. This consideration is for the effects produced by the scientific habits of observation and thought on the internal man, he of the mode two knowledge. The implications of these effects deserve philosophic analysis, and such analysis is of special interest to those who philosophize about education.

Perhaps it is too soon to discern long-range effects. Three hundred years is not a long interval on the scale of human history. It is diminished even further by realization that until recent years only a small number of men could be called scientific. Even they were thinly scattered, and education in science, as we know it, was available in very few places. In contrast, it has been said that ninety percent of all the scientists who ever lived are alive today. When the implications of this remarkable development are joined with those inherent in a national policy which requires that every educable child must have some education in science, the reasons for philosophic inquiry stand obvious.

One point which needs additional perspective is the point at which the modern scientific tradition is said to have begun. The philosophical foundations for physical and biological sciences are frequently attributed to such men as Descartes and Bacon. Foundations for social sciences are found in Kant and in the work of the Americans, C. S. Peirce, William Sumner, William James, and John Dewey. It is a common practice to personify great intellectual movements by attaching the name of the man or men who framed it in the language of philosophy at the time the movement rose to prominence.

Frequently, it is said that the Greeks thought of everything; and, indeed, traces of nearly every modern intellectual or ideological tradition can be found somewhere in pagan or Biblical antiquity. Each man builds what he builds out of what has been passed on to him by his forebears. Men will say, for example, that Newton or Leibnitz "invented" calculus. This is true only in a superficial sense. In a deeper sense this "invention" was merely an improvement on what has been known and used before. It was in a very large part a sequela of man's trial and travail, his industry and zest over the full span of his history. It was an accumulation of the achievement of countless centuries involving even those remote ancestors in the caves of central Europe who were engaged in a struggle to learn how to count.[7] Likewise, the scientific habit of mind is not a sudden invention; it is not an act of total creation. As are all man's consummations, this achievement was built upon generations of experience with and exploration of nature. Although it is possible, as in most things, to name heroes, the heroes came along at a time when men were ready to recognize and appreciate their works. The seeds at last fell on fertile ground.

Therefore, we can recognize in man's initial tolerance of a scientific tradition and in his later full acceptance of it the contemporary effects of an unceasing development of man's nature. There has not been a fundamental change in the sense that man was one thing then and is now something else. Man's inner nature is a scene of perpetual change. Permanence and invariance have no reality except in the romantic musings of the tender-minded, or in static ideals that have only an abstract reality. Man is undergoing endless and universal transition. This is because he is joined by his body to the world of nature, and the forces of evolution surge as strongly within him as in any aspect of life in nature.

But as Huxley has pointed out, the evolution of intelligence has begun. We have good reason to think that man's biological evolution has begun to slow down and that each generation of man has some dimension of mind which was lacking in the preceding generation. In even the brief history of intelligence testing there are strong suggestions that oncoming generations have greater powers of intelligence. Where and why did intelligence begin this evolution? The answers to these questions may not even be answers in the conventional sense of that word. Somewhere, buried in man's past, are factors which

---

[7] Keyser, *op. cit.*, p. 211.

will illuminate the reason intelligence arrived and began its ascendency. We do not yet have the tools of scholarship needed to probe for the location of this massive event, let alone the philosophic insight necessary to understand it.

What can we conclude? What do we understand by this? Science has not wrought a fundamental change in man's nature. Science is simply a recent manifestation of man's changing nature. The biological evolution of man appears temporarily arrested as man's developing nature comes increasingly under the control of his evolving intelligence. What does the future promise? Very little can be promised; man has dangerous tools in his hands, tools which could destroy him entirely or at least send him plunging headlong into the abyss of his own past. On the other hand, his intelligence has arrived at a point where he has begun to understand the genetic chemistry of his own reproduction. If he could assume genetic control and social control of reproduction, his intelligence will be in charge of his further evolution. He could become what he wants to become biologically and intellectually. The potency of this prospect dazzles the mind of a poor Twentieth Century thinker. The future promises nothing to an irresponsible mankind, to a responsible mankind it withholds nothing. Men no longer enjoy the privilege of irresponsibility.[8]

The Adoration of Evidence

The claim that man is not scientific in his nature still holds. Man's nature has constantly changed and these changes manifested first a tolerance, later an acceptance, and finally a developing reverence for the scientific habit of mind. Men have begun to come out strongly for science. But the habits and disciplines which scientific behavior require must be learned. Although man's capacity to acquire and contain these habits or disciplines may be enlarging, science education must install them. Men have an increasing predisposition to be scientific, but science is a part of culture and must be developed in the young. Children still prefer Cinderella and Aladdin to Newtonian mechanics or Darwinian biology. The child's inclination is to think of a scientist as being a magician rather than a man of precision in observation and objectivity in thought.

The point has been passed where an individual can be called educated if he does not acquire some of the characteristics which

---

[8] See Chapter VII.

identify the scientist. The impact of this upon the religious nature of each individual must be considered as profound. Men, even now, call constantly for a demonstration that certain ethical maxims are empirically defensible, particularly if they conflict with personal inclinations. The current rebound from the so-called "puritan morality" of the past is producing demands that self-appointed custodians of propriety and sentiment account for their standards in expressions of evidence rather than in declarations of piety.

Does this mean that evidence becomes a god? No. Evidence is an illuminator of assumption, not a creator of assumption. Evidence can make assumptions tenable or it can make them less tenable. Evidence is food for thought; it does not replace thought, nor does it become thought. Many long-standing assumptions (or beliefs) have been brought into question by evidence. Evidence has provided basis for new assumptions, some of which, very probably, will fall to the ground when even newer evidence is found.

Evidence and Hierarchy

What kind of assumption has not been tested by evidence? Virtually none; that is, none except the assumption that ultimate reality is in the form of an ascending hierarchy of being. For example, it would be difficult to find a scientist who does not value human life above other kinds of life. Extensive and dangerous tests are made on rats, guinea pigs, monkeys, and dogs before techniques involving humans can be applied. This, of course, is not the better scientific way, but it stands as the only way that men will accept for the study of techniques to be used on their own bodies. What can this mean except an overriding belief in the existence of higher and lower levels of being? Ecologists debate constantly on how best to achieve a desirable ecological environment. Desirable to whom? To rats, guinea pigs, frogs, beetles? No. The quest is for an environment most favorable to man and his long-range wants and needs.

It has been only two brief decades since the end of the interval during which the nation of Germany was ruled by a bestial tyranny. During this brief period of extraordinary misconduct, a few scientists of this unfortunate nation were disposed to experiment on fellow human beings. However, even this was not a denial of hierarchy; on the contrary, the assumption of hierarchy was even more vivid. Nazi ideology was imbued with a notion of race supremacy. Non-Aryans, particularly those of Semitic origins, were considered fair subjects for research thought to be of benefit to a "master race." The assumption of hierarchy is horrendous in this application to human life, but it "makes a lot of sense" when it sends dogs and monkeys aloft in rockets to determine the prospects for human survival when the time comes for humans to take their turn at experiencing these conditions. Horrendous in one instance, sensible in another, the assumption of hierarchy is the same in both.

Hierarchy has been with us for so long that it is taken for granted, even by science. It was implicit in Aristotelian physics, and it was made explicit in the metaphysics of Aquinas. It is pervasive of Christian and Jewish dogma and emerges even more strongly in some of the religions of the East. A few challenges exist such as those in transcendentalist literature (the classic challenge is in Coleridge's *Ancient Mariner*). It has been challenged by philosophers in the idealistic tradition, but it has not been challenged by science.

For the most part, scientists go on as if hierarchy is a completely adequate explanation for being. Even though a scientist strives for dispassionate detachment and sharpens his perception to keener edges of objectivity, men of science behave as if man as a being is metaphysically superior to the other life forms of which he has evidence and is therefore of greater value. Who are vegetarians? Who protects the killing of cows? Usually these are men who are committed to religious traditions which originated long before science came to stay.

Science Is Beautiful!

Can a man live in science? Is it possible that he can become so detached that his involvement in social and creature concerns is at the level of necessity only? Apparently it is. For such men science becomes its own object. Science expresses their religious nature; it is their way of being religious. So complete does this detachment ultimately become that hierarchial assumptions and associated values fade to irrelevance. Science is all. The body lives for science; the world turns for science. What of these things are relevant? The body must be kept alive and in comfort. There must be a place for work. There must be freedom for work. The raw and welter of the world is sublimated by encounter with another world, one which contains locus, order, and law. Here in the world of scientific thought is the ecstasy of life. All else is irrelevant. There is not a deity of a conventional kind; there is only the beauty and the wonder which their extraordinary powers of perception and analysis permit their seeing. To such men these things are ecstatic, awesome, compelling; and they are enough.

Such men do not study science in fulfillment of technological purposes. The lure is Platonic. The man chained in Plato's cave[9] could see only shadows of perfection reflected in images on the walls to which his gaze was confined. These moving, flickering images constituted the whole of his reality. Most men, even most scientists, see only this same transient, tentative reality. Perfection is not revealed to him who perceives only the raw physical world. A perfect circle never appears, a perfect triangle can not be incarnated. However much care goes into the effort, some flaw, some mar, some blemish can be detected in the representation. Thus, we are ever destined to see representations only.

But the student of geometry can know perfection in his mind. The idea of a circle is as clear, as exact, and as beautiful as it was to the geometers who sat before Plato and heard his lectures on formal perfection. These ideas are timeless. They have been passed on, intact and unchanging, even by a changing mankind.

How can science be beautiful? It can be beautiful if through it a beholder can postulate a beautific vision, a cosmic vision. Such a vision is not seen with the naked eye, nor is it seen with the amplified eyes of microscopes or telescopes. It can be seen only in the eye of the mind, the eye which views abstraction. A falling star, a celestial comet, a setting sun offer the kind of beauty that is revealed to the gaze of every man. But some men can detect beauty in Newton's abstract mathematical descriptions which illustrate, in ideal form, the mechanical forces by which these events are governed. Indeed, beauty is there; a very profound beauty is there.

A scientist with such powers of mind is very like the man in Plato's cave who has broken his fetters and has in this way acquired the capacity to look around and see the true perfection. With his science he has broken the chain which had bound his perceptions to the world of sensation, and has found it possible to be at one with truth, or near enough to truth that he experiences through his science the deep joy of his life. In this sense he is a devoutly religious man. His secular life is his non-scientific life. For him scientific truth is all there is; nothing is beyond it; there is nothing more. As we are all aware, the world of sensation is precious, ineffably wonderful and beautiful, but it is in the world of abstract conceptions that some

---

[9] Plato, *Republic*.

men find ultimate beauty. For such men it is enough; nothing more is wanted or needed.

Science, Truth, and Hierarchy

Is science the only way to truth? No. Science is a new way of seeking that which man has sought since there came within him the advent of wonder, since he first asked the questions where? Why? Is science the only way to seek truth? No. Plato himself developed a system for truth which gave coherent reason the primary role.[10] Aquinas systematized the method of intuition. More recent views have given weight to ordinary experience or ordinary language. The existentialist position (if the word position is appropriate) is identified by a personalized approach. Is science (or the test of correspondence) the best way to truth? It is the best way only for those whose bend or genius is scientific. There may be many kinds of genius including such types as intuitional, mathematical, philosophical, literal, or ministerial. Each has its own style and achieves its own Olympian view; each develops its own notational style for recording what it sees. Each has its own style for the creation of knowledge. Science is by no means the only way; it is simply one of the newest ways. But for those whose genius is best manifested in science, science *is* the only way. Very few of these can do it in other ways. The Renaissance man was for his time only. Michaelangelo and Leonardo are dead.

Science does not destroy hierarchy. However, in a man whose religion is science, hierarchy is either irrelevant or is tolerated out of biological evidence and social necessity. This affirms once more that the truth the man of science sees does not destroy the metaphysics of hierarchy, it simply fails to give it metaphysical confirmation. Nothing science has done would molest man's tendency to think of metaphysical being as a kind of ladder with all other natural forms of life below man's position and all superior beings above. Science has enabled men to see better that which is below. There is a great profusion of evidence about what is seen there, but although science can help men to perception of ideality in the abstract, science cannot help men to look above, nor can it tell him that there is something there or nothing there. For this reason, the assumption of hierarchy stands.

---

[10] Plato, *The Theaetitus.*

CHAPTER IV

The Fearless Flock

Pity this man who knows himself only
   Within a chanting crowd.
His personal trials are ever lonely
   Society donates his shroud.

DIALOGUE

Student: We have spoken of men whose way of being religious is based upon a belief in the God-idea called traditional theism. We have also spoken of other men who are religious in other ways. What of these men and their God-ideas? Are they aware of their own religious nature? Can they speak of their own God-idea?

Teacher: Those are very good questions. Let us see if we can understand them better. We have said that rational men must found their rationality upon a belief in something. If it is not in belief consistent with the tradition of theism, then it must be in another tradition.

Student: What would such a tradition be?

Teacher: It is commonly said that times change. Have you noticed that the standards by which the public accepts or does not accept the things that men want to do change?

Student: Yes, there are things which used to be considered evil which are not so considered today. It is also clear that the status of women has changed, the moral uses of child labor have also changed, as have the beliefs of many about racial integration.

Teacher: Exactly so. But how can it be that such a thing is true in one time and not true another time? Is it the nature of truth that it changes from time to time?

Student: Perhaps as our knowledge grows we discover error.

Teacher: This may be so in some things, but is it not clear many of these changes are changes in beliefs about things?

Student: Yes.

Teacher: What is it that has changed?

Student: Public opinion has changed.

Teacher: So that some men are content to base their conduct as men on the basis of public opinion or the social consensus?

Student: Apparently so.

Teacher: Thus the group mind or consensus is the source of value?

Student: Is there justification for such a view?

Teacher: There are philosophers who have expressed a belief that God's is man's valuation of the world. It is a form of God-thought called pantheism.

Student: But men do not worship consensus?

Teacher: Not in the conventional sense, but if a man places social consensus in the place God holds in the value structure of traditional theists, the sovereignty of consensus would be recognized in the choices he makes. We could call his obedience to consensus a kind of worship.

Student: Is it possible that a man who bases his values on social consensus may attend religious services which include worship of the Biblical God?

Teacher: What do you think?

Student: I think it is possible.

Teacher: Yes, a belief that Biblical God expresses himself in the race mind or the merged consciousness of man is not wholly incompatible with participation in formal worship services in a church or synagogue. There is a variety of God-ideas expressed in the Bible itself.

Student: Is the view that God is the group mind a recent view?

Teacher: No, such views were expressed in antiquity and were reasserted during the Middle Ages and after the Renaissance.

Student: What form do they take today?

Teacher: In institutions such as the United Nations there is a fascinated concern with world opinion. Political figures are adept in reading its signals. Recently developed social science disciplines are preoccupied with its development. In some places the study of religion is called a social science.

Student: What of men who are not theists who act forthrightly in contradiction to world opinion, what kind of God-idea do they have?

Teacher: Have you noticed that some men are concerned more with the relationships between men than with men alone?

Student: I don't understand.

Teacher: It has been speculated that the relationship between things is of a higher order of reality than the things themselves. For example, the relationship between you and your chair is more real than either you or the chair.

Student: Can it be that the world is really a world of relationships?
Teacher: It has been suggested that the real world is a vast network
           of relationships among men and men, men and things,
           men and institutions, and so forth. All of this is con-
           tained within God who holds a self-relationship to all
           men, things, and institutions.
Student: Is this another God-idea?
Teacher: Yes, each man is a terminal point for a relationship con-
           tinuum which extends in all directions through all men
           and things, reaches God and returns. Such relationships
           are real and alive with interaction.
Student: Then if a man acts in such a way as to alter a relation-
           ship, he alters the world.
Teacher: In this idea, when one alters the "real" world of relation-
           ships he alters something in God.
Student: Then men who are demonstrating or protesting the treat-
           ment they or other men receive are seeking to change
           something in the relationship.
Teacher: They are seeking to recreate the world and by altering
           the relationship continuum they are creating something
           new in God.
Student: Is this religious behavior?
Teacher: What else can it be?
Student: I see what you mean. Are there other God-ideas which are
           held among men which are similar to those two?
Teacher: There are numerous pantheistic expressions which qualify
           as God-ideas. Men base their values and life choices on
           them. Seldom are they identified as God-ideas, seldom
           are they given the status of religion, but men establish
           their manhood and all of their life values on such beliefs.
Student: Are men of such beliefs those who are intent on doing
           good according to these lights?
Teacher: Very often they are and often they do well.
Student: I see your meaning.
Teacher: Do not overly presume my meaning. Such presumption
           may delay your assigning meanings of your own.

POLEMIC

Can you conceive a naked religion? How revolting! What is a religion without a revered founder, without men of contemplative, priestly natures speaking of eternity? No cathedrals or shrines? No bells or smells? How vulgar! Everyone knows that a man, stripped of clothing, becomes a mewling creature who hides in tall weeds and presses his face to the ground. How can there be a naked religion? Without garments, religious belief offends the sight of mankind. A raw belief? Never. We must call it other things, or drape banners over its loins, and pin them in place with words of sentiment. Then a belief can stand bravely forth! Men will turn their faces toward it. They will not be offended. Because now, like a man, it is clothed.

How is religious belief disguised? How is a God-idea called by other things? It simply wears secular garments. Ecclesiastical costume is easily recognized and religious beliefs clothed therein are known to be and are called religious. Some beliefs which have the same effect on the values of men do not wear ecclesiastical costume. They can be found in all manner of dress and answer to various names. Men accept them, live by them, work by them, organize by them, march about in their name, institutionalize them, and develop their traditions in literature. Increasingly, this is the modern mode as men are less inclined toward classical religious forms. The scene of much, perhaps most, of the religious behavior in American people is other than in churches or synagogues. It is in the market places, in the schools, in the legislative assemblies, and in the streets of the cities. We find it in factories and fields, mines and shops, and in offices of medicine, charity, business, and law.

Philosophers would think of the God-ideas which result in such behavior as pantheistic.[1] There are numerous expressions of panthe-

---

[1] See: Josiah Royce, *The Conception of God* (Berkeley: Executive Council of the Philosophical Union of the University of California, 1895; New York: The Macmillan Company, 1898); Baruch Spinoza, *Ethics and De intellectus Emendatione.* Trans.: A. Boyle (London: J. M. Dent and Sons, Ltd., 1913); and various writings on the Brahman and Nineteenth Century American Transcendentalism.

ism. Most of them place God or their God-idea in the world or take the world itself as the God-idea. In some cases the God-idea is a configuration of the ideals of the work in which men are engaged. Craft worship is not new. When it reaches the form of practice the ideals of the relationships (fellowship) among the men are added to the configuration. The God-idea can change as time wears on and the trappings approach the style of the conventional sectarian religions. In fact there are few religious ceremonies which reach the peaks of solemnity achieved by the Masonic and other fraternal orders many of which apply such terms as sanctuary and temple and assert a way of life for members. The fact that in such ceremonies deference is paid to traditional theistic expression changes not the fact that the religious practice focused initially on craft worship and later on fraternalism.

It is not difficult to find pantheism in the deep feelings or ideals men see in their relationships. However, relationships are not the only source for pantheistic expression. Many Americans are preoccupied at a religious level with a problem-to-successful-solution continuum. Others look to group consensus as a source for belief. This is becoming increasingly prominent in value theories of social philosophers and social scientists who sense a high level of reality in man's collective mind.

Fechner, Whitehead, and James are among a number whose theories suggest that God is somehow the union of all consciousness, or somehow "man's valuation of the world."[2] William James wrote specifically of "compounding of consciousness into a group mind."[3] In more recent times a *learned consensus*[4] has been offered as a source for values. This *consensus* is not offered in place of our Biblical God nor is it called God. A suggestion of this kind would immediately be labeled "religious." But if consensus is the ultimate source of values, then it must be God or the God-idea of those who accept its sovereignty. It can not be questioned that such a statement holds powerful religious implications.

John Dewey, certainly a leading educational philosopher of this century, said:

---

[2] Alfred North Whitehead, *Religion in the Making* (New York: The Macmillan Company, 1926), p. 154.

[3] William James, *A Pluralistic Universe* (New York: Longmans, Green and Co., 1909), p. 292.

[4] This alternative was suggested by Harry Broudy in an address at the University of Pennsylvania, Philadelphia, in January 1966.

> There are forces in society which generate ideals. They are
> further unified by the action which gives them coherence and
> solidity. It is the active relationship between the ideal and the
> actual to which I would give the name 'God'. I would not
> insist that name be given . . . (because) . . . any use of the
> word 'God' is sure to be taken as a concession to traditional
> ideas.[5]

Thus, another highly influential view argues that God can have
no meaning outside of human experience and holds that theological
doctrines which rest upon bases external to experienceable processes
add nothing to the meaning of value statements or the validity of a
rule of conduct.

Some of those who establish the divine as a property of experienceable processes are inclined to establish values at the point at which
experience succeeds or does not succeed according to the criteria of
socially developed goals. This is pantheism in action and the mystique
of the consensus is clearly pervasive in this particular form. Awareness of the social consensus is growing. It is often said "we must
appeal to world opinion." The "can't lose" aspect of a peace offensive
is that "rightness" is added to the cause and a "diplomatic victory"
is won. This presupposes that world opinion is for peace. Morality
in international affairs is based upon a conception of the world consensus and not upon standards external to the world.

The late Martin Buber[6] seemed to hold that the world is in
God who holds a self-relationship to all particular things animate
and nonanimate, and He interacts therewith. Though He is God He
is also, therefore, in a state of becoming. Reality is a relationship.
"Primary words do not signify things, but they intimate relations."
Man (I) senses the eternal (Thou) through his relationship (called
I-Thou) with every particular thing in the world.[7] A man does not
turn from the course of his life to seek God because He can be
found in everything. The I-Thou becomes a divine interaction
continuum in which each particular relationship (I-Thou) links
us dynamically to God. We are in a sense living in God and are

---

[5] John Dewey, *A Common Faith* (New Haven: Yale University Press, 1934),
p. 51.

[6] Charles Harthshorne and William Reese, *Philosophers Speak of God*
(Chicago: The University of Chicago Press, 1953; Phoenix Edition, 1963), pp.
302-306.

[7] *Ibid.* Quoted from Martin Buber, *I and Thou.* Trans.: R. G. Smith (Edinburg: T. and T. Clark, 1937), p. 3.

ourselves partners with God in the work of creation, and because reality is the totality of relationships, we are also joined with God in creating something in God.

If the world is in God, and reality is relationships, and the relationships have their terminal points one in man the other in God, then God interacts with man through this extended relationship (I-Thou) and can be, therefore, deferential to man's will. If this will is demonstrated decisively, God's appreciation of the world can change; and, thereby, reality is altered. Decisiveness combined with humility registers on the divine.

With this understanding, such widespread public movements as the civil rights crusades become religious rather than merely social. Demonstration of collected wills has the religious purpose of altering reality. If the relationships between men are changed then the world has changed; it becomes something other than it was. Non-violence, therefore, can be far more effective than violence. Non-violence can change relationships; whereas, violence hardens them. Force, even successful force, from the viewpoint of its usual objectives, can do no more than establish the conditions for new relationships. Until relationships have changed, no new value is registered on the relationships which constitute the reality of the cosmic community.

Thus, we have religious behavior which has only incidental relationship to orthodox religious conduct. It is studied in school in courses called social studies, civics, history, problems of democracy, and English. Group processes are an important part of teaching method in the elementary school. This is not religion ungarbed. It is religion in secular clothing. It is not immorality; it is morality on another standard.

What important concerns grow out of understanding pantheism as a kind of "unofficial religion"? The first is that we must cease thinking that education in the direction of group thought or human relationships is devoid of religious content. This kind of religiousness may be in or out of ecclesiastical costume; only in philosophy is it stripped of covering. Only a small portion of any public sees it thus exposed. The second is to note that such doctrines have wide and growing appeal. They seem to prosper best where social action intensifies. Urban rather than rural settings offer the best prospects. The third is that pantheistic ideas tend to be antithetical to hierarchy and distinction.

In government the leaders still go to church on Sunday. But as the days of the week pass by they constantly consult the consensus.

Right action is that which will gain the greatest long-range approval of the electorate. Democracy itself implies a limited pantheism although democratic processes have an adequate base in other views of man and in other God-ideas.

The Utopian writers of our own century, most notably Huxley and Orwell, have formulated dark views of the ultimate consequences of this super-social morality. Bastions of privacy and personal enterprise are assailed by such precepts. They move, as has been constantly implied, in the most humane of garments. But it is clear that such doctrines hold no special place for the individual man and his personal God. Mankind is not a body of existing individual men. "No man is an island" the meditation goes.[8] Mankind is a flock, a cluster, which makes its own rules, and changes them with impunity. As an individual, man knows fear. In the flock, there is no fear except fear for and of the flock. If one must have fear, perhaps this is the best kind of fear to have. All would be well if we individuals could be certain that on the occasion of the ultimate confrontation between the individual and his creator, the flock would be there too.

---

[8] John Donne, *Devotions Upon Emergent Occasions, Meditation 17.*

DISCOURSE

Let's All Sing Together

The idea that God is or is represented in the group mind deserves more attention from American educators. Recently, anthropologists have noticed the strikingly religious overtones of the football game ceremonies conducted by American high schools and colleges.[9] Although they may vary from place to place there is little reason to doubt that these Friday evening or Saturday afternoon rites may be the most significant religious experience of the week for some of those participating, and for those who have no other religious exercise, it surely fills a need. We only need to look at what transpires as one would who came from a distant and alien culture and who sees us for the first time.

There are drums pounding out a throbbing parody of the rhythm which dwells deep in nature. The drummers syncopate their drumbeats galvanizing a mood of excited anticipation. The feeling grows that a many-chambered heart has taken over the life-giving function for the whole of the crowd. Its beating is welding all into one. (Those who march to the beat of a drum are different men.) Then the young, fertile maidens appear, bottoms up, at last possessed of a socially approved reason for wearing revealing costume. The primitive traits of animism make their presence felt in the form of the incarnated spirit of a lion, a tiger, a bear, or an Indian. Very often, as he passes, the cheerleaders fall to the ground in mock reverence and adoration.

The moment of truth approaches, as the players confront each other, passions aroused. This, too, is a tautophony, a refrain of time

[9] Professor Ray L. Birdwhistell, anthropolist of Temple University, noted the strong semblances between American college and high school football games and primitive religious ceremonies at science writers' briefing in November 1966. His observations were quoted in a syndicated column by William Hines which appeared in the public press on November 8, 1966.

immemorial. The players stand ready to sacrifice themselves to the group god. This, of course, is not as open or as direct as animal or human sacrifice, but the sentiment runs true. The Greek games took the place of this kind of sacrifice, and the winners pleased the gods. The difference here is that the religious nature of the ceremony is felt but is never called by the word religious.

From beginning to end this mysterious cementation goes on. The crowd is brought to chanting, exhortation, and mass frenzy. The lusty clamor is stilled as a player is stretched upon the ground twisting in pain or lies there ominously still. But quickly the attendants whisk him from view, and the lust begins anew. When it is over the individual man regains his solitude with a feeling that for a little while he was part of something bigger, something apart, something which mattered very much. It was real.

If such a scene were observed in any of the so-called primitive societies at any point in time, we, ourselves, would readily think of it as religious. However, in our own culture it is simply a game, and so it is. But is it just a game? If it is, then why all the fuss? Possibly the most overly simplified expression used in education is "school spirit." What kind of a spirit is a school spirit? We have known for a long time that such exercises have a profound effect on group identification and loyalty. It appears that what we strive for whether in games, concerts, or graduation exercises is this groupness so vital to the continued well-being of the institutional order.

Bravery of the Flock

Philosophers who speculate on the group mind have, as one might expect, produced different theories. William James, the American philosopher-psychologist, seems to have endured extensive personal distress in reconciling collective consciousness with the existence of God.[10] Out of his anguish was born a conception which seems to make mass mind an aspect of God. James apparently conceived that there was much more to consciousness than awareness. The consciousness extends beyond existential awareness.[11] Man is not completely aware of all that he is. (Substantial support for this has arrived in the form of recent experiences with drugs. Unfortunately, those disposed to licentious applications obtained possession

---

[10] Horace Kallen, *The Philosophy of William James Drawn from his Own Works* (New York: Modern Library, n.d.), p. 29.

[11] James, *op. cit.*, p. 313.

of them before disciplined research produced decisive knowledge about the nature of effects. In one case, there is good reason to think the drug destroyed the researcher.) James apparently thought that at some point beyond awareness consciousness merged or interlocked with others. Through this interlocking consciousness we are led to postulate a race intelligence, a philosophy of race mind. This postulation is not entirely new, but its implications for a developing mankind are constantly new.

Are men all components of a single intelligence? If so, how does this intelligence manifest itself in relation to men? In a school there is a consensus which forms among students about the school itself. When student loyalty is high, when that mysterious thing called morale is high, students support the school and its faculty and administration. When the opposite is true, the school has problems in its operation. Group experiences of all kinds affect the student consensus about the school. Consensus goes beyond school. There is a community consensus about the school and other things. There is a national consensus; and, as men have become aware of each other on a global scale, there is a world consensus.

A ceremony in which individuals are joined by common garments, marching, physical exercise, chanting, or singing produces emotional effects in the individual which bring him to fuller communication with the group mind. Drugs, as it has been implied, may do something similar. Inspiration is gained from this communication, loyalty grows, and in some cases a kind of psychological fulfillment results. We can call any ceremony through or by which an individual transcends his ordinary level (or condition) of being a religious ceremony.

This is particularly true insofar as the group mind or the consensus is a source of values. Here we give the group mind a Godly role. We offer to it the status of God even though we are not prepared to claim it is God. Hence, any ceremony which is designed to bring the individual into meaningful communication with the group mind and its hierarchy of values is an agnostic religious ceremony. It is agnostic in the sense that it makes no pretense of knowing what the divine is, but by its very nature it acknowledges the presence of something larger than man and operates to communicate with it. The divine and the good are felt by the heightened awareness of the way in which the individual consciousness or each mind is merged and unified with the group mind.

Thus the flock becomes brave, and men do brave things if their deeds are consistent with what the flock wants and needs. There is a blessed assurance in feeling that the group mind approves. It is a temporal god or a temporal aspect of God. If it is the former, it is pantheistic; if the latter, it is panentheistic. James apparently tended toward this latter view.[12]

One may well ask, why do none of the modern religions make use of games? Christianity, certainly the foremost among the organized religions of Western civilization, had to overcome the pagan religions which at that time were sustained in part by the very appealing tradition of athletic contests derived from Hellenistic culture. The connection between paganism and athletics was not soon forgotten. The Christian tradition was not only gameless, but because many of the pagan games glorified the human body, the church, until recent years, appears to have opposed the exposure of the human form. However, the Olympics have begun again. At the outset of each quadrennial renewal a thinly clad runner brings down the holy fire from Mount Olympus in a flame-spouting torch, but it means nothing. Or does it?

This agnostic groupness is pantheistic and seems also to turn man toward paganism. Men are no longer encouraged to act as individuals. To have meaning at all a man must identify himself in some kind of group. To be heard at all he must be heard through a group. Thus, there is a great proliferation of organizations. Indeed, it appears there are more organizations in the United States than there are people. The credibility of this assertion emerges if one takes the time to enumerate all of the groups to which he belongs or with which he is involved. If a reasonably healthy, active American is not prominent in the hierarchy of at least one organization he is either actively resisting or socially unacceptable.

Is God world opinion? If He is, then the United Nations is one of the foremost of our religious institutions. It may be more effective as a guide to religious attitude than if it had a more direct kind of political, economic, or military power. Although a world organization does not express values for local community life, it can generalize to the whole of mankind and furnish a vital forum for further development of general human values. It is interesting to observe the relationship between two world organizations such as the United Nations and the Roman Catholic Church. The one is an organization of nations which seeks solutions to the problems of temporal life. The other

---

[12] Harthshorne and Reese, *op. cit.*, pp. 335-352.

is a supernatural organization composed of men who are increasingly struggling to solve the same problems. What does the United Nations "think" about population control? What does the Church "think"? Until recently the Church took the position that it was immune from error on such questions; now the Church appears increasingly deferential to the collective voice of man.

The Reality of Relationships

It was said that philosophers differ about their speculations on group mindedness. The implications of the speculations of Martin Buber are of increasing importance to American educators. In his theory of relationships we find correspondence with another kind of social behavior which is seen in school and community life. The bonds between man and men and men and God are also unseen but they are of a different nature. Buber's thought seems to give a greater role to the individual while at the same time withholding from the individual a private, personal, or independent reality. Man is, but he is not alone, and this is the fundamental aspect of his reality. In fact, he establishes his reality as he establishes his relationships with all other things, through them to God, and with God directly. He becomes the totality of all he is related to.

In this theory the teacher must see that the individual is constantly relating to God in all that he does. In this framework there can be no non-religious activity. Activity can only be more or less religiously decisive. For example, if students strike for institutional privileges, this is not rebellion because in such a conception rebellion is impossible. The students have a relationship with the institution and its authorities and they seek to alter it or invert it.

Men do not turn from the course of their lives to find God. God is found through every relationship. Relationships are infinite in nature. They sprawl both ways into time because the future and the past of any relationship are inherent in the present. Relationships among people open new worlds. Imagine a young woman whose adolescence was characterized by interest in art, music, literature, and, of course, young men. None of the young men in whom she was interested was athletic by nature or by inclination. So she emerged into womanhood knowing little and caring less about baseball. However, her first child was a lusty, brawling boy who in the course of events became a Little League shortstop. Now we find her on summer evenings atop the bleachers shrieking malevolence at umpires, exhorting the Little League players to greater enterprise, using the abrasive jargon of the game as if she had spoken little else since birth. What happened?

We know of the relationship between mother and child. The very continuation of the human race depends to some extent on that relationship being what it is. Often we use the word "love." In this case, love is a noun. Love is the thing that exists between the two. What has this relationship done? It has opened the child's world to the mother. She is involved. The relationship with the child brings her into a world which is composed of the child's relationships. In turn the child relates to other children and their relationships. The chain comes back to the mother.

If we accept this view of reality, what is implied for education? Certainly it would mean that we would seek to understand more than we do about the qualities in all relationships. One would expect to see a school devoted to the graphic, literary, and performing arts presided over by sensitive teachers dedicated to the task of refining the child's feeling for relationships to levels approaching Sapphic intensity. Religious education, therefore, would tend toward development of the rhapsodic rather than the reverent man. Only the man deeply sensitive to infinity and eternity of his relationships could find God.

The familiar journals of William David Thoreau furnish an example of a man who found deep meaning in his relationships. A stroll alone across a country meadow would provide substance for hours of contemplation. Can education develop in man such a gift for observation, sensation, feeling, and experience? Or is such a thing the consequence of inborn genius and known only to other men because it is expressed to them through language? In either case, the potential is there. The man deeply moved through love of nature and love of man is having a religious experience in the experience of this love.

Gnostic or Agnostic

Pantheism in American life, or, more particularly, in American education offers at least two important opportunities for religious experience. The first is through the interaction with a group mind, or the resolution of identity in a social *milieu*. This can be achieved through the processes by which society establishes and sustains values. Any experience which weds the individual more closely to the values established in the social consensus is religious in its nature. The second domain of opportunity is in developing deeper sensitivity and insight into things and people through the intensification of the feelings inherent in every relationship.

The question arises whether the exercise of either of these opportunities results in a denial of the God of our Biblical heritage. The answer appears to be that it does and does not. How can this be? The explanation lies in the difference between *pantheism* and *panentheism*.[13] If God is world opinion or social consensus, that, and nothing more, then God is in the world, has only a temporal nature, has not knowledge of Himself, and knows the world only through man's cognition. This is an outright form of pantheism. It is not atheism because there is a belief in the reality of a divine force. Although there is a belief in this divine force and an acceptance of its value manifestations there is no profession of knowledge as to "its" nature; in fact, there is downright resistance to having "the force" discussed in anthropomorphic terms.

On the other hand, some accept the belief that *social consensus* or *world opinion* is an aspect of God's reality which is *in the world* even though God is also apart from the world. Although God has this temporal quality (world opinion) He is also eternal. In addition He knows He is God and He knows the world and man's problems. Such a conception as this is sometimes called panentheistic. The form of pantheism which simply resorts to group mind, world opinion, or social consensus as the God-idea is also a form of agnosticism. In this category the divine is accepted but no claim of knowledge of the divine is made. In fact, the assertion is usually made that knowledge of the divine is impossible. Panentheists, on the other hand, are gnostic, they can accept world opinion as an aspect of God's reality, but are quite settled in their acceptance of the revealed nature as taught in the traditional view.

The same possibilities exist for those who seek God through relationships. Pantheists sense the divine but tend to be agnostic because of a tough-minded resistance to precise definitions of God's nature. However, Buber himself, though considered a phenomenologist, went beyond the usual boundaries of agnosticism in defining the nature of this relationship (I-Thou) and in depicting God. Buber's speculations would disturb only extreme gnostics such as those often described by the word "fundamentalist." Although a phenomenologist,

---

[13] *Ibid.*, p. 1.

Buber's speculations, if taken to the point of objectifying God, must be classed as metaphysical.[14]

In the School

Probably most of the school activities which could be called "religious experiences" because of their power to produce internal commitment to social consensus or group mind are extra-class activities. The football games, assembly programs, pep rallies, mock conventions, music programs, and certain forensic activities all have this potential. Social science courses produce a rationale for an intellectual approach to this God-idea. There is no evident reason to claim that these activities as they are conducted promote either gnosticism or agnosticism. However, insofar as they can be satisfying religious experiences it appears reasonable to assume that agnosticism will emerge if gnostic ideas are either not presented, seldom presented, or treated with derision as so often is the case. This writer is not taking sides in the matter but wishes, at this point, to persuade his colleagues to understand this view of the problem and consider the implications it holds for the religious development of American children and youth.

In the humanities (and this, as it turns out, is a word full of mystery) we promote the sensitivity to relationships. Humanities programs can have other goals, but to the extent that some humane teaching has as its purpose the deepening of perception, the intensification of sensitivity, and the accretion of involvement, these experiences are religious and the content of such teaching is religious content. Again this is not to make it seem sinister; this is only to identify it for what it is and to reduce the masquerade. If this writer is neutral for anything, he is neutral for the increase of the humane curricula and humane teaching.

Again, there is nothing inherent in the humanities which promotes either gnosticism or agnosticism. But it also seems obvious that those who prefer a gnostic solution to the ultimate questions have the worst of it in an educational environment which forbids the presentation of traditional religious views in their best form. The problem of values is immensely complicated by this kind of environment. The visibility of a rationale for traditional morality and traditional authority on moral problems is decidedly reduced. At the same time we urge a higher in-

---

[14] *Ibid.*, p. 306.

tensity of experience, and we think of this as a good. We urge every man to indulge a deeper relationship with every other man regardless of race, color, or creed. We want a profound compassion for the oppressed so that we all share the pain, the strife, and the despair of crushed aspirations. No one can guess where all this may lead except that we hope for no pain, no strife, and the end of man's inhumanity to man. We probably should hope for less pain, less strife, and less inhumanity, but it is absurd to accept these things as being man's ultimate purpose. One central theme of this treatise is that man is purposeful in his nature. Life, as William James once said, may not be a struggle *but it certainly feels like a struggle*. Can it be that it is in man's nature to struggle?

When a man is educated for a greater intensity in relationships, among those things intensified are his goals or aspirations. Also intensified are his strivings for those goals and his doubts and uncertainties about their reality. A Christian or Godly humanist may be far more at peace with himself and his fellow man than the worldly or Rabelaisian humanist. The latter has no "bed of roses" in life. Of the great masters of the English language few can match the efficacy of John Donne in observation or expression. His life presents something of a model for contemplation on this point. At the peak of his power he was a worldly humanist in the most classic sense. But as that power began to fade with advancing years, Donne began his retreat to the certainty of the gnostic solution.[15] It is a common course which many lives follow. The greater the struggle, the greater the need to find and accept a moral base for the world. Every man is entitled to whatever peace such a discovery would bring. Would we not aid the quest each child must make if we were certain that all the alternatives are before him? Yes, each man must draw his own map, but this can be better done if he is privileged to view the charts which other thinkers have drawn to reveal the trails followed in finding their own ultimate reality. No signficant solution should be withheld on the fatuous and irrelevant grounds of civil law.

Implications? Let us try to understand more of these things and go on with the problem.

---

[15] From an address by Glenn J. Chistensen on the life of John Donne entitled *Retreat to Certainty*. Chistensen's point is that as Donne's physical powers faded and death became iminent he retreated to the gnostic solution.

CHAPTER V

Man Alone

Devotion is our dearest enemy,
  Paradox is our dread.
The mind's not made for bigamy
  Doubt only can we wed.
But the success of process rings
  With truth for those who find
Meaning abides in working things
  Not in the life of mind.

DIALOGUE

Student: We have said some men have the God-idea that there is no God? Are not such men often very firm in this belief? And do not we call them atheists? How can atheists be religious and how can this kind of believing serve to shape values?

Teacher: Are there not bodies of knowledge studied in school which do not admit of supernatural explanations?

Student: Yes, biology is such a subject; so are the other physical sciences.

Teacher: Do they deny supernatural explanation?

Student: It is not a question of denial. One is simply compelled to make his observations sovereign to his feelings or beliefs.

Teacher: Very good. If observation stands counter to feeling or belief then the feeling or belief is not true.

Student: But some time ago we said that hierarchy can be seen in nature and there is no good reason to suppose that man is the highest point and that other forms of being stand above him as do the several that stand below.

Teacher: Was hierarchy of being observed or assumed?

Student: We found differences in levels of existence, did we not?

Teacher: We found differences but was it not assumed these differences represented levels?

Student: Then our discovery of hierarchy was only made possible by supplying an assumption to what was observed.

Teacher: Yes.

Student: But does not observation make the assumption reasonable?

Teacher: Yes, but a belief in that which is not observed is still required, and science forbids the exercise of such a belief in the operation of its knowledge systems.

Student: Such forbidding and demanding, disciplining and denial are aspects worn by religious practices.

Teacher: Have we not suggested that scientific atheism is a religion?

Student: But why do we so often consider science to be a denial of
           religion?

Teacher: Is it not the custom of any new religion to deny the cen-
           tral elements of its predecessors?

Student: Perhaps so.

Teacher: Are there knowledge systems that examine men and their
           feelings?

Student: Is this what psychologists do?

Teacher: Some of them do and in this century a number have
           advanced brave new theories about feelings that men have,
           including their feelings for God.

Student: What theories?

Teacher: In general, that God as a supernatural being was created
           by men to fill a void of one kind or another.

Student: Such as our failure to understand ultimate reality.

Teacher: Yes, that, and to offer other kinds of security needed for
           hazardous ventures or even in the personal rigors of com-
           mon life.

Student: This suggests that man created God rather than the other
           way around.

Teacher: Yes, God becomes something man has formulated into a
           useful force in his personality. Such theories hold that men
           are capable of creating useful illusions which continue as
           delusions. Some have suggested that the delusion of a su-
           pernatural God turned into a race neurosis which men have
           only recently begun to overcome.

Student: Do these say that God is dead? Is this what they mean?

Teacher: Some of them mean this when they say God is dead.

POLEMIC

Life builds and owns its own house. Then why do men speak out for a builder and cry out for a landlord? The purpose of life is to create life. Life is its own purpose! It needs no external urging or restraint, guide or model. Every natural event has a natural cause. Each day we witness life as an event in nature. Therefore, its cause must be somewhere in nature. We will find it! These excursions in search of a super-nature are mere diversions of fools and mystics. Reality is sensation; it is experience; it is problems! When men know these things they know life, and this is enough life for anyone who will face it. Why do men torment each other with other things?

There is no God! All can be accounted for in the fullness of time. Energy, the fortuitous combinations, the accumulation of mass, the interaction of unlike elements, these contain the secrets we seek. What is time? It is perceived motion. All is relative to the perceiver. This order we see and sense, is it there? Or is it imagined, spun out, as Bacon said, of the juices of our own bodies. Indeed, the cosmos may not be cosmic; it may be chaotic. The cosmos comes out of the head of man. He imposes it on all he perceives.

What kind of God-idea is this? What metaphysical category? It is an idea that there is no God. It is atheism. How then can it be a God-idea? Does not the umpire of a baseball game call balls and strikes. Surely he does not call strikes and non-strikes or unstrikes. A ball is not an umpire's version of a category of strike. It is a ball and a ball has its own categorical definition. But the point is not in the differences between ball and strike; the point is in the throwing of a pitch. This pitch could either be a ball or a strike (it must be one or the other) but it remains a pitch and the umpire will say the pitch was a ball or the pitch was a strike.

Likewise a God-idea is a God-idea. If that idea is that there is no God an umpire of ideas would call it atheism. If the idea is that there is a God, the umpire of ideas would call it theism or pantheism, depending on the details of the idea. In baseball both balls and strikes are pitches. In philosophy both theism and atheism are God-ideas. An atheist's God-idea is that there is not a God of any kind.

This is a central part of the whole problem. The atheist has considered the reality of God and he simply rejects the idea that God has reality. Moreover, he can be very passionate and highly devout in his rejection. It would be very easy to support the claim that some of the most devoutly religious of the American people are atheists.

A highly devout atheist has a number of ways of reflecting his religious posture. Only one of these can be to combat theism in any form. One would readily suppose that an atheist would be primarily inclined to ignore the religious exercises of believers in God. Most atheists are so inclined, and few of them are heard from. The few who are heard from are militant in their convictions. Some of these will resort to legal proceedings to prevent, wherever possible, the development of a public environment wherein theism is a prominent influence. They argue that such an environment is hostile to atheism and conducive to theism. As such it offends them or the aspirations they hold for the religious development of their children. Therefore, the legal crusade undertaken by an atheist is actually a religious crusade in the fullest and most classical sense of the term.

Such legal-religious crusades succeed and prevail because of the highly interesting and probably unintentional structure of law which was instituted in the dawn of our national life. There is probably no question that the founding fathers who approved the non-establishment amendment did not conceive it would be used to create a climate for atheism. The public schools, as we now know them, did not exist at the time and many of the elementary schools and a high proportion of the secondary schools were church dominated. Today, many are convinced that the founding fathers would find some current usages of their legal structure to be anathema. But these forebears of ours have no ways of making their views known as specific matters, and speculation about their views would be a form of disrespect!

A climate for atheism must be at least as injurious to theism as a climate of theism is injurious to atheism. Appeals to atheists to exercise some tolerance for the majority religion have, for the most part, been granted. However, in American jurisprudence only one atheist can, by legal recourse, impose his will not only upon the majority religion but upon fellow atheists as well. The American people must consider whether their commitment to religious freedom (because theism is denied to the schools) is greater than their commitment to individual rights. Suppose a Catholic or Protestant child attended a school where all other children were atheists. Could the parents of the child sue for his right to pray?

Atheism is felt and taught in school in a number of ways. For example, the *a priori* foundations of biology and psychology are atheistic. This is as it should be. Such disciplines require of the scholars a rejection of supernatural categories or explanations. This rejection is consistent with atheism. Many, probably most, scholars in these disciplines are Godly men in the traditional sense. However, the disciplines, as they stand, are influences toward atheism except where seen in the context of the Thomistic traditions (see Part III).

The Scopes trial in the late twenties focused upon this problem. The teacher was convicted and, in the strictly legal sense, the conviction was correct. However, the conviction was incorrect in terms of the requirements the field of biology places upon its researchers, students, and teachers. The important concern here is that the (religious) atheistic thrust of biology be re-identified and recognized for what it is. Whatever else it may be, it is a definite category of God-idea. The religious behavior of a first-rate biologist *when he is being a biologist* is in the tradition of atheism.

Counseling is another area of interest in this regard. Some modern counseling theories are based upon Freudian, Jungian, Sartreian, Nietzscheian, or Rogerian precepts which also are or tend to be in the atheistic tradition. But we must be clear about this. In the counseling of students, atheism is not presented nor is it discussed. One is never told there is not a God. There is no need to do this. The *assumption* of no God is pervasive of the counseling theory and of its applications.

In counseling situations God may emerge as a force in personality or as a sanctuary from certain kinds of problems. Some counselors see the evangelical Christian (or evangelical anything!) as a kind of sadistic personality who has seized upon God as an instrumentality for aggression upon others. It is suggested by such counselors that the idea of God serves this purpose admirably because the aggressor's aggression is disguised by the cultural presupposition of goodness. Masochistic behavior tends to draw opposite responses. Counselors will often report that a counselee is undergoing self-flagellation in the spirit that God is punishing him. In some ways these and other counseling attitudes can produce an assertion that a counselor who is devout in an orthodox sense is in some sort of emotional difficulty.

In regard to counseling, the Twentieth Century appears to be the reverse of the Nineteenth. In the latter, if one wished to enter counseling he trained for the clergy, and he studied philosophy and psychology. In the present century, one who aspires to counsel frequently finds his training dominated by applications of psychology, sociology, and anthropology. Today, one can hear the clergy say they do not feel properly qualified to counsel. Such self-doubt is not expressed by the new group. They are the new priesthood! Their God-idea has yet to face its most serious challenge.

Oh, to live in the Twenty-first Century! This age of tomorrow will view all of this with Olympian detachment. They will compare the counselor style of the Nineteenth Century with the counselor style of the Twentieth Century. We cannot write their verdict, and—more's the pity—we can never read it.

DISCOURSE

The Nature of Atheism

Critical comment has been directed at this writer for his insistence upon calling atheism a religion and for referring to atheists as religious men. This is not unexpected. The weight of tradition in philosophical discourse is against such a portrayal. Great writers of the past dealt extensively with the dichotomy of religion and non-religion as if it were not only real and profound but also highly vivid. Nietzsche posed as an archenemy of religion. But how can there be an enemy of religion if there is only religion and no other side? Are we saying that Nietzsche was a fool? Jean Marie Guyau wrote of the non-religion of the future.[1] How can non-religion have a future if non-religion is impossible? Was Guyau also a fool? Some American pragmatists have written of religious men as if religious men were someone else. For centuries theists have written about non-religious men and have worked to convert such men to the side of religion. Was all of this also foolishness?

Of course not. In the past the circumstances of life, language, and law were such that it mattered less how the word was used. Until the present century most formal education was in the hands of non-public institutions. Indeed, church organizations were in the forefront of most major educational enterprises. Even in the philosophic discourse of today, the word "religion" stands innocent of implications beyond its long-standing connotations. However, when the discourse moves into the fields of law and education, any interpretation of the word "religion" has a resounding impact. The possibility that any distinction which gives separate reality to non-religion may be, in the ultimate, philosophically indefensible deserves immediate attention. One of the central ideas in this treatise

---

[1] Jean Marie Guyau, *L'Irreligion de l'avenir*. Trans.: *The Non-Religion of the Future* (New York: Schoken Books Inc., 1962. Printed from original version of 1887, trans. to English in 1897).

is that a distinction of this kind is fallacious and harmful, and atheism offers a case in point. However, an assertion such as this swims upstream against the currents of tradition in discourse. It has not been undertaken lightly by the writer and should not be regarded lightly by the reader.

There is, however, a growing tradition for this broader use of the word "religious." It seems clear that religionists such as Tillich and van der Leeuw tended toward this view.[2] Eckhart in urging the presence of religion in the university acknowledged the existence of a view that religion is implicit in man.[3] Kahil Gibran expresses it in the towering eloquence of his poetry.[4]

In the ancient contest between theism and atheism the word religion has been a bystander, but it has never been supposed as a neutral bystander. Theists have been commonly regarded as religious. Atheists or antitheists have been considered to be non-religious. However, the main issue between the two was whether there was or was not a God, independent of creation and possessed of the qualities of love, wisdom, and holiness. If a man came to a belief in such a God his commitment was understood to be religious. If a man came to a belief that there was not such a God his commitment was understood to be non-religious. Here is the point at which the error begins to appear. On both sides there is *belief;* on both sides there is *commitment.* Therefore, instead of religion and non-religion we may have polarized religious positions.

However, this alone is not enough to show atheism to be a religion. To do this it is also necessary to expose *the nature of the belief* and something of the way it is *expressed* in *feeling* and *action.* To what lengths must an atheist go in order to establish his atheism? Atheism is not merely antitheism such as might be sensed in pantheism. It is not merely *unbelief;* it is *disbelief.*[5] In some ways a disbelief is harder to achieve than an unbelief. Disbelief is *denial* whereas unbelief can be considered as *failure to concur.* This distinction can be real; and, in the case in point, such a denial requires its own act of faith.

---

[2] Martin E. Marty, *Varieties of Unbelief* (New York: Holt, Rinehart and Winston, 1964), pp. 123-124.

[3] Roy Eckhart, "Is There Anything Religious About Religion"? *The Journal of Bible and Religion,* Volume XXXIV (October 1966), pp. 303-304.

[4] Kahil Gibran, *The Prophet* (New York: Alfred A. Knopt, 1923), p. 77.

[5] Robert Flint, *Anti-Theistic Theories* (London: William Blackwood and Sons, 1879), p. 6.

An oft given example[6] is that of a man who comes ashore alone on a quiet tropical island. On his first look about he finds animal tracks which extend across the sandy beach. From this evidence he fairly concludes that there is or was animal life on the island. On the other hand, let us suppose that evidence of this kind would not be found. If he finds no tracks in the sand, or any other evidence of animal life, our castaway could conclude or believe that he did not know whether there is or was animal life on his island. However, it would require an infinitely greater search, one consuming months or years by one expert in reading all the signs before there could be a conclusion that there is *not* and *never was* animal life on the island. Such a belief would require *faith* that all of the possibilities were seen and had been examined and implies faith that no other possibilities exist. In addition, the believer must have faith that his senses and his reason have not deceived him. Such a negation is possible but only if the believer invokes these elements of faith.

This analogical reasoning is not intended as an argument. Its purpose is to illuminate the atheist's faith in his own omnipresence. One can not easily arrive at a faith in his own omnipresence.[7] To do so he must believe that he has seen all there is to see, heard all there is to hear, and thought all there is to think which is relevant to his conclusion that God does not exist. He must also feel assured that his senses and reason are correct. Only after having overcome all of these very formidable obstacles can he truly pronounce his denial or disbelief in God. With all of that faith in him, who is there that can say he is not religious?

Various kinds of atheism can be identified. The example here is of the extreme category which is often called *absolute,* or *dogmatic atheism.* It was selected because of its capacity to dramatize the internal commitment atheism demands of its believers. As has been claimed elsewhere in this treatise, all begins in doubt. A man chooses his own base of certainty. One who makes an absolute denial of God is at the end of doubt; he has arrived at a certainty.

Nothing could be more certain than the denials of Nietzsche or of Marx. There is no doubt in the words of Fuerbach who wrote, "There is no God; it is as clear as the sun and as evident as the day there is no God, and still more that there can be none."[8] There is

---

[6] *Ibid.,* p. 9.
[7] *Ibid.,* p. 12.
[8] *Ibid.,* p. 7.

ringing certainty in the attitude of Gustave Flourens who proclaimed, "Our enemy is God. Hatred of God is the beginning of wisdom. If mankind would make true progress, it must be on the basis of atheism."[9] Such adulations require a faith as sturdy and robust as that professed by the most devout of the Godly men.

Philosophers, if they please, can call such vigorous disbelievers non-religious. Churchmen, if they please, can think the very suggestion that such men are religious to be irreverent. But schoolmen know the fury, impatience, and intolerance with which they come on. The absolute atheist is hard to satisfy. The situation is made much more difficult because his status as non-religious extends him the favor of the law.

Kinds of Atheism

In religious literature, atheism is frequently denounced but seldom examined. The term "atheism" as used here applies to all thought systems which are opposed to theism. There are numerous systems which have alternatives to the classical forms of theism, but only those theories which refuse to acknowledge even the existence of a God are atheistic. Even so, it is a wide field which deserves more scholarship from students of philosophy, religion, and education. How can one study a denial? When one affirms the existence of God he presents support for his affirmation in the forms of revelation, reason, or direct evidence. However, when one simply says that he does not believe, the believer goes on the defensive or proclaims the non-believer to be a misfortune both to himself and mankind in general.

Atheists have always been a minority, frequently an oppressed minority. As such they have little reason to examine each other. By contrast, until very recently, believers in God have had little peace with each other. Opposing views have produced proliferation of sects which have competed in many ways. With all of the fine points at issue among churches, it could be said that all they had in common was an aversion to atheism. From time to time they have been more or less inclined to tolerate it, but seldom if ever has there been much inclination to seek an understanding of it. Even though such writers as Etienne Borne[10] find the field quite extensive, religious literature seems to contain very little research on the kinds of atheism which

---

[9] *Ibid.*

[10] Etienne Borne is a French Catholic student of atheism and author of *Atheism.* Trans.: S. J. Tester (New York: Hawthorne, 1961).

exist. In the midst of his contemporary problems, the man of the Twentieth Century will come to regret this defect more as time goes along.

The *absolute atheist* has already been identified and discussed.[11] He is one who regards God's existence as anathema. Moreover, he is aggressive in the ways open to him to defeat the presence of God in the thoughts of men. Prior to the present century the only ways open were in philosophy and teaching or in the exercise of private power as, for example, the head of a family, a property owner, or an employer. In recent times, as indicated above, he has discovered his favored position in the law and has invoked his legal prerogatives in the spirit of religious freedom. This paradox has been described.[12]

If all atheists were called to say what it is they would put in place of God it would soon be discovered that they would have a great many sects, perhaps as many sects as are found among the believers in God. In addition to the absolute atheists there appears to be a second kind of atheism which we might call *humanistic atheism*.[13] There are several varieties of humanistic atheism. These are known by such words as Promethean humanism[14] and Rabelaisian humanism (or worldly humanism). All of these forms of humanistic atheism tend to "co-exist" with theism. It tends to lure the believer away from his steadfast theistic position. It seldom makes a direct attack upon theistic ideas. Fuerbach seems to be more in the humane style of atheism despite his frank declaration, of God "there can be none." Humanistic atheism is more in the spirit of unbelief rather than disbelief.

In general, humanistic atheism elevates man to an absolute. He is, indeed, "the measure of all things." The humanistic atheist feels he can not accept God without diminishing himself. If we think of a man as whole, complete, and possessed of an independent essence, then God becomes impossible. In order to have God man must be incomplete; man must relinquish part of his essence to God. In the eyes of a humanistic atheist a man worshipping God is doing no more than

---

[11] The absolute atheist is also of the class called dogmatic atheist.

[12] See Chapter IV.

[13] Humanistic atheism is a term chosen by the author to cover several traditions in atheism.

[14] The term *Promethean humanism* appears in Robert H. Beck, *A Social History of Education* (Englewood Cliffs, New Jersey: Prentice-Hall Inc., Foundations of Education Series, 1965), p. 3.

However, Beck does not associate the Promethean tradition with atheism. He tends to associate it with liberalism in thought.

worshipping his own relinquished essence.[15] When it is called God, however, this relinquished essence is idealized and seen from a distance. The human blemishes are obscured. Fuerbach makes the point that to enrich God man becomes poor. If God is all, then man is nothing.[16]

The Promethean humanist finds himself consistent with this point. Prometheus, the titan of Greek mythology, in sorrow and concern for man who was weak and helpless among the creatures, determined to enrich man by the divine gift of fire. Such a gift made man more god-like, and because of this, the gods were diminished. In their wrath they punished Prometheus by chaining him to a rock. But never again was man weak and helpless and never again were the gods so great. The flame itself became the symbol of man's ascendancy.

The atheistic humanist sees man as if he were seeing through the eyes of God. He gives up no part of his being; he relinquishes none of his essence, and he withholds nothing from himself. However, in the Promethean tradition *man cares about man*. In this tradition are found the elements of respect for man which are so important in the construction of Kant's moral imperatives. It is well to note the differences implied by the words "respect" and "love." The Promethean humanist seems to dwell more on respect and considers respect as the more appropriate conception of the ideal human relationship.

The Rabelaisian or worldly humanist is a different tradition which is often personified in the French monk who turned physician. There is a flavor of naturalism. There is more of the *epicurian* influence and less of the *stoic*. To the worldly humanist man is a child of nature. He is not, as is the Promethean humanist, inclined to project divinity into his own nature. He considers man as one peering out from the skin and tissues of an animal. Rather than revering his own nature he revels in it. Rather than thinking of man as *divine* he considers him *amazing*. Rather than thinking of life as a tragedy he sees it as comedy.

A third variety of atheist is the *skeptical atheist*. The skeptical atheist demands the criterion of empirical truth. This category of atheism is mainly the companion of science. In this tradition, no proposition is self-evident or is fitted to carry conviction at once

---

[15] James Collins, *God in Modern Philosophy* (Chicago: Henry Regnery Co., 1959), p. 243.
[16] *Ibid.*

to every mind. There are certain tests to which it must submit, certain standards it must meet. Inevitably, there are two levels of acceptance. The first level is that of demonstrated certainty. Assuredly very few propositions survive at this level, and the proposition that God exists is certainly not one of them. The second level of acceptance is at the point evidence suppresses doubt. This level adjusts itself according to the importance of the action contemplated. In the vast majority of the practical affairs of life if one hesitated to act until he had absolute demonstrated certainty he would do very little at all. In fact, he would never move. We are inclined to act when doubt is suppressed even though it is not overcome entirely. Although judgment is not final, the need to act calls for a judgment that is best in terms of the action needed.

It is appropriate to say that skeptical atheism is a mode of unbelief rather than disbelief. The skeptic is at someplace between his reverence for the criterion of empirical truth and his need for or feeling for God. So long as his beliefs are under the control of the criterion of empirical truth he remains a *skeptical* (or *critical*) atheist. However, in his private problems the feeling or the need for God ebbs and flows. At any point he may experience something which brings him to an active belief in God. If the need or feeling is strong enough he will not wait for absolute certainty.

A fourth category of atheism is often referred to as *naturistic atheism*. The knowing naturistic atheist is one who stakes his life on processes. Essentially he is a *methodologist* (not to be confused with Methodist). He is "tough minded" about reality. He thinks of man as an observer of and participator in a process that is producing perpetual change. The basic proposition is that nature is all there is; there is no more. There is process in nature; man is part of nature; there is process in man; man is part of society; and there is process in society. In such thinking the understanding of processes will lead to everything which can be known about whence man has come and whither he is going.

Although there is not a tendency to deny religious experience, personal religious experience has a psychological explanation. Social religious experience has a sociological explanation, and so on. Men of this persuasion come to understand their purpose in terms of biological and psychological drives. They even find process or method in man's attempts to evade life processes. For half a century the popular literature has been full of accounts by psychologists which describe men who are ill because they are attempting to evade or compensate for life-drives. Even the illnesses are systematic: Paranoia is this, melancholia is that, and so on. How do things tick? This is what they want to know; this is the question at the base of many of the recently developed knowledge systems. But what man wants to understand is why do they tick? What happens to them when they cease to tick? These questions are not the concern of the naturistic atheist. Knowing "how" will tell him all he can know about the cause and course of the world. The "why" and "wither" are unknowable.

Technical analyses can produce numerous sub-classes of naturistic atheism. They are identified by such terms as "materialism," "instrumentalism," "pragmatism," "antidualism," "pluralism," "positivism," and there are others. Each is related to a more detailed and more specific expression of naturistic atheism. The more precise meanings of these terms is of great interest only to the specialist. However, the generalist needs to understand that naturistic atheism includes a range of believers from those who are openly hostile to a belief in God to those who are merely unempathetic to God.

The final category which is discussed here would probably contain the largest number of people. This category has been suggested by Robinson, Flint, and Maritan among many others. It is *practical atheism.* In the interests of simplicity the practical atheist can be described as a man who professes belief in God, even thinks he believes in God, but whose *actions* constitute a denial of God. In other words, he *says* and *thinks* he believes but *he does not* believe. For example, his church can be a practical way of accomplishing a great many practical things such as making friends, securing business or professional connections, and gratification of other autistic interests. Proclaiming belief in God and professing "proclaimed belief" may be a way to gratify an inclination toward aggression (or sadism) and to do so in a "holy cause." We can suppose that many aggressive people find such a "belief" admirable for this purpose. Few people will think other than good of them even though they are invading and intruding upon the privacy of others.

It is a complicated, heartless, and highly presumptuous thing to suggest to a man that his profession of belief in God is instrumental to another purpose. One would be well advised never to do it. However, we can do no less than think that a number of such people exist. It is not a semantic trick which has made them atheists of this kind. It is plain in the things that they do that the values which govern their choices are antitheistic; therefore, we can not think of them as theistic regardless of what they say.

The point of this discourse is that the word atheism covers a great variety of beliefs. Much more scholarship is needed to develop a taxonomy of atheistic concepts that would be useful for students of philosophy, religion, and education.

Apostles of Atheism

It is not only unusual but somewhat cruel to suggest that many Sunday school programs sponsored by American churches are apostles of atheism. They certainly mean to be the opposite of this, but an aversion to God is the inevitable result when the teaching typical of most Sunday schools is mixed with the other components of the education of the modern child. A Sunday school does not become an apostle of atheism by direct intent, and no aspect of the child's school curriculum is atheistic by intent. But atheism is inherent in many of the things that are taught or done in school, and the atheistic tendencies produced in school are aggravated and not subdued by the approach of the typical Sunday school.

How does one become an atheist? It has been stated[17] that atheists are various in kind. Some are absolute, others humane, some are skeptical, others naturistic, and most are practical. It has also been indicated that one becomes an atheist by religious choice.[18] The religious choice he makes is a result of his interacting with all of the religious alternatives he understands and selecting (either consciously or unconsciously) that which forms the most satisfactory basis for the syntax of his values.[19] His God-idea may answer to any one of a variety of categories, but it should surprise no one if a modern church-going child who attends a typical public or private school should select and accept one of the atheistic systems for his God-thought.

This is not an attempt at critique of American church education; this writer has not the qualifications for such an undertaking. It is necessary here only to cite the inappropriateness of beginning religious education by reciting miracles. It is sheer folly to begin the religious development of a modern child by presenting him with information that he will, at some later point in life, come to look upon as incredible. The greatest losses to theism in America probably occur as consequence of the disillusionment that youth experience in early adolescence. At this same time the ideas of atheism and pan-

---

[17] See "Kinds of Atheism."
[18] See Chapters I and II.
[19] See Chapter II.

theism are in the youth's environment and they exert a powerful appeal. He learns to laugh at countless St. Peter jokes and "preacher" stories, and he finds himself yielding or not yielding to inclinations which place his churchly idea of God alongside his sentimental childhood memories of dragons, ghosts, and Santa Claus.

This is too bad. The maturing theist never had an opportunity to view his developing belief in a rational perspective. What kinds of things are included in a rational perspective of theism? The assumption of hierarchy is one. The assumption of a "prime mover" is another. The expectation of a moral purpose or base for the world is another. There are other metaphysical postulations consistent with a belief in theism which are as rational as those consistent with other beliefs. It is unfortunate, for those who prefer the theistic solution, that at the point in life when the maturing theist should make his leap of faith he begins to doubt the ground upon which he stands. His picturable, anthropomorphic God of miracles becomes less and less believable.

By contrast, atheistic concepts inherent in the school curriculum appear highly credible. One discipline which in and of itself denies extra-natural reality is biology. If a biology teacher makes no effort to the contrary, he can produce in his students a greater inclination to atheism than he himself may have. Students have been known to express astonishment upon learning that their biology teacher is a devout, church-going man. Biology, like any other discipline, has a number of rules which its scholars must follow. The *a priori* foundations of biology are atheistic in both the skeptical and naturistic tradition. Many biology teachers in failing to make a distinction between the rules of biology and the metaphysics of life become unintended apostles of atheism.

Any course in literature is freighted with a great variety of God-ideas. Atheism is well presented. One would expect those who write so well as to become paragons of their language to have extraordinary sensitivities. Their feelings about God as well as most everything else are subtly conveyed in their work. This has long been recognized by the church. In particular, the Catholic church has invoked restrictions on what children may read as an indication of its standing concern for the influences of literature on God-thought. There are many, this writer included, who are convinced this is not a good way to deal with the problem. It is far more general than just those books on the Index.

To be sure there are Godly humanists such as Dante, Mallory, and Erasmus, but these had their near contemporary counterparts in Chaucer and Boccaccio. The fun-loving Elizabethians had a wide range of interests which must have inspired Shakespeare's extraordinary capacity to reflect the Rabelaisian spirit in his comedies and the Promethean spirit in his tragedies. This same range of interests made a fertile bed for the Shakespearian overtones of mysticism and fate in dealing with the base and the inspiring, the ignoble and the noble. Is that a glorification of the autistic alternative? Of course not. It is simply the vivid painting of values derived from sources independent of theistic systems. Panentheism finds expression in the works of Coleridge and Wordsworth who seemed to sense a divine unity in all creation. Wordsworth apparently considered man and nature as different manifestations of the same creative power, both animated by the same divinity which is eternal yet temporal, in the world yet more than the world. His solution is suggested in *Tintern Abbey* where he envisions a divine:

> Whose dwelling is the light of setting suns,
> And the round ocean and the living air,
> And the blue sky, and in the mind of man:
> A motion and a spirit, that impels
> All thinking things, all objects of thought,
> And rolls through all things.

Promethean humanism reaches a climax in Shelley who, it seems, never permitted his personal disillusionments to destroy his faith in the perfectability of men. The atheistic elements inherent in his work are seldom developed and probably never urged by teachers. It is simply there. He remains only a "blithe spirit" deeply preoccupied with the pagan musings of the golden age, an iconoclast in a deep revolt against the institutions of the Christian era. In Act III of his *Prometheus Unbound* he places these words in the mouth of Jupiter:

> The soul of man like unextinguished fire,
> Yet burns toward heaven with fierce reproach
>   and doubt,
> And lamentation, and reluctant prayer,
> Hurling up insurrection, which might make
> Our antique empire insecure, though built
> On eldest faith, and hell's coevil fear;

On this side of the Atlantic, American authors wrought an equally wide range of God-ideas. Some of the most brilliant American writers were in a kind of revolt against the iron-handed Calvinism of colonial New England. Hence, from the Unitarian and Transcendentalist movements we have expressions which tend to put theism in its worst possible light. Nathaniel Hawthorne's brilliant, gripping, but improbable *Scarlet Letter* depicts the New England Calvinists as a gloomy and superstitious lot. Although he does not show them to be evil they nevertheless emerge from his pages as coarse and heartless. They may well have been so.

However, it should be remembered that the Puritans were a tiny group attempting to impose civilization on a wilderness. They made strong demands upon themselves and upon each other. It is unfair to judge them by contemporary standards. It is also unfair to hold up these hard-bitten, severe moralists as examples of theists. In the parlance of today, Puritan morality is increasingly reviewed with derision. Some today wish to define their hedonistic outlook and licentious conduct as a revolt against Puritan influences. They should find better philosophic ground than this. After all, what was Puritan morality? They did manage to perpetuate the race and transmitted other values which have been great sources of strength in America's past.

In modern times a tendency for authors to create Bible-quoting villains can be easily detected. Television programs have depicted the inherently evil "bad one" as one who knows the Bible well and quotes it when the "good ones" question his conduct. The child on one hand is led to think the Bible is a source of moral precepts. Yet he is entertained in his home by stories which associate the Bible with evil. What implications does this have for his choice of God-idea?

Villains have quoted the Bible and Puritans were overly severe with those who violated aspects of their moral code. It is proper these truths be presented in literature. It is also proper that this literature be taught in school. But the influence of such material must be examined. It must not be taught out of balance. If we believe that our children deserve the freedom to choose theism, they must have clarification that religious commitment to the God of our Biblical heritage does not imply villainy. Modern theists do not have an interest in reincarnating the morality and ethic of the Seventeenth Century New England colonists in a modern suburban community. (It would be an interesting thing to try!) There is little reason to go on beating this kind of theism into the ground. The point has been made.

Other voices in American literature offer alternatives to classical theism which are also taught in the school. The powerful insights of Thoreau and Emerson reflect both naturistic atheism and panentheism. Emerson's mighty concept of the *oversoul* is one of the most profound God-thoughts in American letters. It implies a pantheism reminiscent of the Brahmam of the Eastern religions. Though it is shrouded in mystery, "Always our being is descending into us from we know not whence," it is also a positive vision which sees the world as "the perennial miracle which the soul worketh."

A more thorough disclosure of God-ideas in literature is tempting but beside the point. There can be no question that the content of our literature has powerful religious implications, and, if the literature is well taught, these implications will register strongly on the students. It is relevant now to look at other aspects of the student's life in school. In particular, the work of educational counselors should not evade attention. Counseling is a significant development in modern education. Teachers have always been involved in giving students advice about academic, vocational, and personal decisions. Within the present century, however, this work has been formalized and professionalized. Even so, teachers are still expected to do much of it. Only complexities are reserved to the professional counseling, and the guidance counselor is a fixture in secondary education. Now these professionals, joined by certain lay elements, are engaged in a movement to install professional counselors in elementary schools.

Counseling theory is a mixture of a great many things too numerous for adequate exposure here; however, it is clear that counseling theory is dominated by the *new* behavioral science knowledge systems. There is a widespread acceptance of the taxonomies of personality aberrations. On the other hand, there is disagreement about whether a counselor is a prescribing clinician, a teacher of values, or an empathizer. Although *measurement* is a strong concern in the counselor field, the clinicians appear to be losing ground. Counselors also seem disposed to shun identity as teachers. Guidance appears to be growing in the idea that the counselor is a non-directive empathizer who offers support of an individual in his encounters with his "phenomenal" field. (For purposes of clarity here it is only necessary to think of a child's phenomenal field as his problem-ladened life. To a specialist it is a more grandiose conception.)

There are numerous questions about what role the counselor takes in developing values. Occasionally theoreticians will suggest that the counselee rather than the counselor dominates the counseling environment. However, it must be recognized that whether the counseling situation be directive, non-directive, or mixed, decisions are worked out and choices are made. Therefore, regardless of who dominates, counselors must accept their involvement in developing values and shaping religious nature. Even if the counselor manages to remain neutral in his own eyes, he must recognize the influences cast by his presence.

How far should counseling go? Some theorists assert that counselors should remain at the problem-solving level. Others argue that counselors can and should penetrate the ego level and work in the reconstruction or redevelopment of personality. This gets very complex, and it raises a host of questions for which answers are not presently at hand. However, there are signs that counselors want to go deeper. This, along with their growing interest in elementary school children, makes it even more vital that the philosophical inclinations and presuppositions of professional counselors be examined and discussed.

For example, there are metaphysical inclinations inherent in the present style and content of counselor training. This training tends to be dominated by behavioral theory and psychologically developed techniques. If counselors intend to enter the world of the student to the extent of participating in the reorganizing and revaluing of his personality they should furnish their minds better with all the religious concerns of man. They need some training at least in both philosophy and religion as intellectual disciplines.

This writer is not in a position to understand whether or not counselors should enter these deeper waters of ego development. How could anyone know this? There are certainly a great many children who need and want this kind of help from someone. And someone should help them; counselors are the most logical of the available alternatives. However, it would be wrong to take this step without fundamental changes and extensions of their preparation.

If theism is to remain open as one of the God-ideas which might be chosen by a student, it is important that counselors come to an acquaintance with counseling theories which do not look upon a child's commitment to traditional religious forms as a source of anxiety or guilt feeling, or which regard responsibility to God as a pseudo-concept, or which regard the world as indeterminate, and free of extra-natural influence, or which structure the goals of counseling upon *social aims* alone. If counseling is to be bigger, then counselors must be bigger. This appeal does not rebuke propositions that school counselors assume a stronger role. It merely argues that counselors who counsel in depth must understand that there are important and defensible views of reality which not only rebuke the present foundations of the counselor's art but deny them entirely.

CHAPTER VI

Prayer in Religious Education

In beauty men find victory
  O'er evil's aggravate
Its ideals stand interdictory
  Against an aimless fate.
Find God and Beauty in ideal
  Expressions of the love
Which binds man to an empyreal
  Blazing summons above.

DIALOGUE

Student: Our venerated judges have said that we may be taught about the ideas of God which are based in our Bible. They have said we may study the Bible so long as it is not treated as a Holy Book. We may discuss the God of our Biblical heritage if we do not pray to him. Does this not make it possible for the presence of this God in our schools to be stronger than ever?

Teacher: Are we certain of this? We have found that even this God may be approached intellectually, but He can not be accepted without some effort which results in a faith, a belief, or a conviction.

Student: This is true, and is it not possible to achieve such an internal feeling through the kind of study which is found in school?

Teacher: Perhaps it is. But let us consider the academic style which is characteristic of our schools. Do our schools tend to concentrate on what children can become or upon that which children can do?

Student: On things they can do.

Teacher: Do the achievement standards speak more of performance than of attitudes, beliefs, and so forth?

Student: They do.

Teacher: Would you say that our academic style in regard to beliefs is that they should be accepted or questioned?

Student: I would say we learn to question beliefs.

Teacher: Do you suppose a course given in the way a usual course is given will lead to convictions that the God of our Biblical heritage exists?

Student: There is no reason to expect it would. In reality, it would make God appear academic and in a class with other phenomena which are examined in this same way.

Teacher: Do you mean that such study could work against a belief in the God of our Biblical heritage?

Student: Yes.

Teacher: I tend to agree with you. For centuries men have taught that this God can only be studied and known through prayer. Academic discourse may not be the way to arrive at an appreciation of God which approaches religiousness.

Student: Do you mean this requires another environment or an appeal to inner feelings?

Teacher: It could be that God can not be studied at all outside of religious experience which recognizes Him as God.

Student: What does that mean?

Teacher: It means that any study of the Biblical God which is not predicated on acceptance of revelation, application of prayer, and a deference to His Holy Word which places it above the level of literature is apt to be ineffective if not debilitating or damaging.

Student: This implies that the academic style is bad?

Teacher: No. It simply claims that academic experience is not the sort of experience which leads to the choice of the idea of God inherent in traditional theism.

Student: It is an interesting claim and possibly valid.

Teacher: But one which our judges have ruled unlawful.

Student: A senator from the land of prairies and quiet rivers wishes this law to be changed so that prayer can be given or undertaken by those who so wish. Is this good?

Teacher: Do you think that a man should be free to choose from among all of the God-ideas?

Student: Yes.

Teacher: If he is to be free to do this, must not all God-ideas be equally open and available to him?

Student: Yes.

Teacher: This means that each should be represented in its best form?

Student: Yes.

Teacher: And we have found there is serious doubt as to whether the academic style is the fairest exposure to theism. In fact, have we not shown it as possibly unfair?

Student: Yes.

Teacher: Then is there complete freedom to choose?

Student: No.

Teacher: And this is wrong.

Student: I believe it to be wrong.

Teacher: Then you must have sympathy for what this senator is trying to do.

Student: I want to think about it. The problem is much deeper than I first thought.

Teacher: So deep, in fact, that you may want our laws to allow children to pray in the schools?

Student: Yes. It may be that the judges have been wrong about our laws.

Teacher: Their problem was difficult and we should not judge sincere men with difficult problems except in their sincerity.

Student: Are they sincere?

Teacher: Yes. The problem is now in our hands; we must make new laws if we don't care for what established laws provide.

Student: I am very interested in what the senator is trying to do.

Teacher: So am I.

POLEMIC

Shall we take a course in Christianity and become Christians? What nonsense! A new epistle is needed. The great apostle must be reincarnated. We must again have the wrath served to the Corinthians. Let Paul write to the Washingtonians. Paul's letter to the Washingtonians—what would it say to those Washingtonians who wish to teach the Holy Book as a work of literature? How many nouns? How many verbs? See the beauty of the metaphors! Would he teach a course in Jesus? Ah, Washingtonians, you want sounding brass and tinkling cymbals; you see through the glass darkly! One does not study Christ in the academic style.

What did the brooding Kierkegaard say of Christianity?[1] It is historically absurd. It is the only great religion whose founder can not be approached historically. Shall the teacher lecture to the children of a man called Christ whose mother was a virgin and who arose three days after his crucifixion? Is this how we shall study such a God-idea? It can't be done. No, we shall have films. There will be background music which is inspiring, but undistinguishable from that of any church. The film will show a man on a mountainside telling people that the meek are to be blessed; they shall inherit the earth. What an interesting idea! We shall discuss it in social studies! The film will go on; the speaker before the multitude will be saying his concluding words:

> And in praying do not heap up empty phrases as the Gentiles do; for they think that they will be heard for their many words! Do not be like them, for your Father knows what you need before you ask him. Pray then like this—Our Father who art in . . .[2]

---

[1] Kierkegaard was preoccupied in his *Fear and Trembling* and many of his other writings on Christianity and Christendom with the necessity of the Christian to overcome absurdity through faith.

[2] Matthew 6:7-9.

And the film will switch to another scene, men around the table eating lamb, bread, and wine. They will be handsome, graceful men, not those who wear aspects of fishing or farming. In the background a voice will be explaining the various mechanics of the Trinity. He will discuss the Christian Mass and will use words such as "transubstantiation" and "consubstantiation." Soon there will be a test, and the school will be proud because it can be proved that students know more of these events and these theories than any students any time before.

The students will take a trip. They will get aboard great yellow buses and ride to a church. The teacher will say to them that they are on a field trip. Into the cathedral the girls and boys will go, and the girls will giggle about putting something on their heads. Didn't Paul say that women should cover their heads . . . ? The priest at the door will explain the figures on the windows; he will take them down the long aisle explaining more things as he goes along, the altar cloth, the rail, the dishes, the cross, and all the symbols. The students will ask questions, and all will be explained. The priest will be proud of his explanations, and the teacher will think how fine his young people look, and a tall slender sensitive boy in the group will hear in his head the words of Nietzsche:

> . . . even Gods putrefy. God is dead! God remains dead! And we have killed Him. How shall we console ourselves, the most murderous of all murderers? The holiest and mightiest that the world has hitherto possessed has bled to death under our knife—who will wipe the blood from us? With what water will we cleanse ourselves?[3]

The students will board the bus and the teacher will thank the priest. Both in their hearts will be proud of their cooperation. Surely this will lead to better and greater things. The driver will be instructed to return to the school. From his window seat the boy will look upon the cathedral and hear more of the words of Nietzsche:

> The deed is as yet further from them than the furthest star— *"and they have done it."* It is further stated that the madman made his way into different churches on the same day, and there intoned his *Requiem Aeternam Deo.* When led out and called to account, he always gave the reply: "What are these

---

[3] Friedrich Nietzsche, *La Gaya Sciencza.* Trans.: Thomas Common, *The Joyful Wisdom* (Edinburg: The Darien Press, 1910), p. 168.

churches now if they are not the tombs and monuments of God."[4]

Why must the laws of our land kill this God? Teach him in a course, and fulfill the gleeful prophecy of Nietzsche. What better way is there to convince our children that He is nothing more than a race neurosis from which we are at last released. *"And we have done it."* Teach of Him and His church in our academic style? How can we keep all we show and all of which we speak from appearing as a relic or paraphernalia left over from a madness of which we are recovered? Shall we study it as we study numerology, palmistry, phrenology, and astrology? It is another dead religion the moment it comes into the hands of a secular teacher. *"And we have done it."*

Perhaps we can be more profound! The great seminarians could be brought forth to teach in schools. Surely, it might be reasoned, the presence of great scholars of religion will impress the children and the youth. Men of great intellectual power are always respected and admired. Respect and admiration are elements of adoration. Adoration of men of God can be the beginning of a religious life. But hear the words of Kierkegaard:

> Passages are to be found in the New Testament which justify bishops, presbyters, and deacons (however little the present examples resemble the original picture) but one will search in vain in the New Testament for a passage where professors of theology are mentioned . . . "The Professor" is a later Christian invention indeed, for it was made about the time when Christianity began to go backward and the culminating point of the "The Professor's" ascent coincides exactly with our age when Christianity is entirely abolished.[5]

We can not be didactic and we can not be profound. This God is studied through prayer! He comes to man as an inner response to an inner effort. One does not abstract Him; one finds Him and surrenders to Him. It is a passionate surrender. It is an objectification of the will. It is the taking on of a new life. Nietzsche called the man who sought God "a madman." ("I seek God, I seek God.") It was those who would not seek God and who laughed at the man who was seeking who were called the killers of God. Let us understand this

---

⁴ *Ibid.*
⁵ Soren Kierkegaard, *Christian Discourses*. Quoted by Walter Lowrie, *Kierkegaard* (New York: Harper and Brothers, 1962), Volume II, p. 508.

better. A religious education which is not *characterized by a seeking of the God of the Christian faith* will not produce a Christian. Such an education may produce a religious man but, as we have said, he will be religious in other ways. The love of Christ and the love of man are not found in a classroom exercise, even if that exercise is in a church classroom.

Is the judgment of the judges immoral? In at least one sense it is. If existential man is entitled to free choice among the alternatives of God-ideas we must then register a claim that the God-idea of traditional theism is denied appropriate access. More than this, the court has advocated practices that will place it in a most unfortunate light. This is particularly true of the God of the Christian faith. The moral demands of existentialism can only be met by an educational environment which offers equal favor to theism, pantheism, and atheism. The developing environment of public education favors the latter two and disfavors theism. In this sense, the judgment of the judges is immoral. The God of the Judeo-Christian tradition is denied his full presence in the free market of ideas to which our children come daily for their lessons about life and values. Anything less than a full presence is more harmful to Him than no presence. This is what they are doing. *"And they have done it themselves."*

Shall we deplore these atheistic and pantheistic religions? Shall we strike them down? Drive them out? No. Indeed, no! To do so would be immoral. As religions they have great appeal. They, too, have shown themselves capable of giving vision and vitality to men. Have they not survived persecution? There is no reason to deplore them. We can even call them good, but there is an even higher good and that is the freedom which assures the continuance of all religions.

What then can we deplore? Surely there is something to deplore! Let us deplore the denial of freedom! Oh, Washingtonians, whose freedom do you deny? You have denied freedom to the God of the Christians and the Jews. Wherever the business of government is to be done, He must leave. This is no small thing! The business of government is everywhere. Look about and see. In all of these places other gods enter with impunity. But the God of the Jews and Christians can not come as God into the places where government does its work. Is this not a denial of freedom we should deplore?

But the Christian God is omniscient. He rules. Does not the potter govern the clay? Did He not say, "You shall have no other gods before me"? When He is present, other gods must leave. Does not He then deny other gods their freedom? Christians, here is our dilemma!

We protest that our government denies freedom to our God. But if our government accepts His Godly Presence in schools are not other gods required to depart therefrom? Denial of freedom to the God of any man is wrong. Washingtonians! You have our sympathy.

Can we change the nature of this Biblical God? Will He adjust to the requirements of our law? Change the nature of God! How presumptuous! Oh, Billy Sunday, are we not His people? He created us, why then does He not change us? Or our laws? Or even our government? The stars were in His heaven before they adorned our flag.

Yet still there are changes. It seems the nature of God has changed. How changed? The diggers at Tell es-Sultan have uncovered the rubble of Jericho. At the command of Yahweh the sons of Israel came forth from the wilderness of Kadesh to slaughter all that lived in that hapless town saving only a harlot named Rahab.[6] Later this same God bade his servant Saul to "Go and smite Amalek and utterly destroy all that they have, and spare them not; but slay both man and woman, infant and suckling, ox and sheep, camel and ass."[7] What kind of God was this? He spoke to His people from a mountain, like Zeus from Olympus. He made His people instruments of his anger and retribution. He was a God of war, pleased by the sacrifice of enemies taken in battle.

His people carried Him in the Ark of the Covenant into the valley of the Canaanites. He competed with the Baals for territorial sovereignty. He was enshrined by those whose fate flourished with the crops. He called upon His people to celebrate the Feast of the Unleavened Bread, the Feast of the Tabernacles, the Feast of Weeks, and the Feast of Harvest. Did not the rites to encourage fertility of the soil later turn into sodomy and prostitution? But the swords were to become plowshares and the spears, pruning hooks. He was, indeed, a changing God.

He became a God of the sky, crossing many lands even into the bellies of the great fish of the sea. He spoke to individual man. He stood apart from the lonely, suffering Job and listened with detachment to his bitter questions. Then he praised Job for his questions! And he rebuked Eliphay, Bildad, and Japhar who counseled Job in orthodoxy. He called upon Job, the man, to stand up and be a man. He told him to apply the power of his mind to his problems and with this "right hand" he could save himself.

---

[6] Joshua 6:25.
[7] Samuel 15:3.

> Deck thyself with majesty and excellency
> And array thyself with glory and beauty
> Cast abroad the rage of thy wrath,
> And behold everyone who is proud and abase him.
> Then I will confess unto thee
> That thine own right hand can save thee.[8]

This God followed His people into exile, comforted their misery, inspired and protected their prophets. Then He seemed not a God of storm, wrath, and war, but a "Universal Spirit everywhere available to the seeking soul." The hard justice and firm retribution were softened by grace and forgiveness. Ideas about Him began to multiply. To the Hebrews He was righteousness and will, One who performs mighty acts within the world process. There was a Divine plan, a Divine community, and people with a Divine heritage chosen by God for God's purpose. Further north, Aristotle led pagan thought to a conception of an unmoved Being in which there is ultimate unity and rest. Later still, Jesus taught that He was the Father of man, and He placed God's authority behind man's love of man, man's love of God, and God's love of man.

In the beginning man looked up into the mountains; later men looked into themselves. These are distinctively different kinds of searching for a distinctively different God. Did God change? Or was early revelation wrong and later revelation right? Or is revelation progressive? Is it true that the more God is revealed the less mistaken we are about the Truth of His nature? In the early days of his seeking, man found a god of battle, intent on bloody triumph, commanding slaughter of the innocent, inspiring violence and fear, denying succor or mercy to all but a few people. In these later days of man's seeking He is found to be a universal Father who abides in love, who is the redeemer of every child of every tongue, who abides in love, and who is the ultimate hope of man for brotherhood and endless peace.

Has God really changed? Is He, like man, maturing and civilizing Himself? Who can know this? However, men have always sought this God whether they looked to the tops of mountains or into themselves. If revelation is progressive, then it might be man's Divine purpose is to go on seeking God in the certain faith that each generation which renews the quest will see Him more clearly than those which searched before.

---

[8] Job 40:10-14.

Can it really be that a man who stands in a place the public owns, in an attitude of prayer, searching for God through a meditative merging of his outer consciousness with his indwelling mind and spirit is committing an offense against those who have chosen for themselves another god and are content with this other god? What nonsense! Can it be that a child who stands upon public property, searching for God in the best way men have ever known to conduct this search is breaking a law which commands his government not to establish a church? What nonsense! The judges can not mean this, but it has happened.

It is good that a church can not fashion a prayer for all children. Likewise, it is good that a government can not fashion a prayer for all children. It is not good that a child in need of fashioning his own prayer can not be helped either by his church or his government during the long hours he is *required* to spend in perhaps the most vital learning environment of his life. All must come to terms with God. We must realize that some do this by prayer. This prayer is not merely the practiced mumbling of remembered words. Prayer is the deep, reflective search for unity with God. Has a child, a youth, or a man no right or opportunity for a school experience of this kind while other gods roam the corridors and classrooms with impunity? What irony!

How ironic it is that we mount our attack on the poverty of man by feeding him knowledge while consenting to the continued starvation of his spirit.

> By the rivers of Babylon there we sat down
> Yea, we wept when we remembered Zion.
> We hanged our harps on the willows in the midst thereof . . .
> How shall we sing the Lord's song in a strange land?
>
> —Psalm 137

DISCOURSE

The Paradox of Christianity

Christianity is an ecstatic religion. In its authentic form it relies on pervasion rather than invasion. Its high expressions are the ideals of forgiveness and salvation, peace and love, communion and unity. Although it may be the object of rational inquiry, the reality of Christianity is the reality of emotion and not the reality of reason. In almost all of the theistic religions, man seeks God. This is also true of Christianity, but Christianity differs in that God is also seeking man. When unity is achieved the experience is ecstatic and is resolved in salvation. Jesus said: "I am the door, by me if any man enter in he shall be saved."[9]

Christianity is also a *paradox*. Often the word *hypocrisy* is used, but paradox is much better. Paradox is a kind of "ore" out of which philosophers refine meaning. Hegel, for one, was fascinated by paradox and his fascination is reflected in his version of the dialectic. In a geometric sense, paradox can be taken to mean that two things which contradict each other are found to be occupying the same spot. When the contradiction is illuminated by philosophic analysis, the contending elements of the paradox take on separate and often new meanings. Old confusion may disappear (and, sometimes, new confusions appear).

The elements of the paradox are Christianity and Christians. The paradox here was once highlighted by someone who said, "It is possible to love Christianity and to hate Christians." Gibbon estimated that Rome, in all of its history, in all of its provinces could not have martyred as many as two thousand Christians. He was highly conscious of Rome's infamy in this regard because he concluded his finding with this gratuitous observation:

---

[9] John 10:9.

We shall conclude this chapter by a melancholy truth which obtrudes itself upon the reluctant mind; that even admitting, without hesitation, all that history has recorded and all that devotion has feigned, it must still be acknowledged, that the Christians in the course of their intestine dissensions have inflicted far greater severities on each other than they had experienced from the zeal of the infidel.[10]

Thus, the flame of paradox grows even hotter and higher in the realization that not only have men hated Christians, but history shows that Christians have hated Christians with such rigor as to give the chronicles of man some of its liveliest passages. These were Christians but there was little Christianity in them.

Gibbon, an historian, and Kierkegaard, a philosopher, are but two among a multitude of scholars who have called attention to the fact that Christianity can not be defined as that which men called Christians do. Kierkegaard once declared, "the fundamental misfortune of Christianity is Christendom . . . Christianity is literally dethroned in Christendom." Organizations of Christians face the paradox when they understand that the very existence of their organization requires that upon occasion they perform acts which are anti-Christian in character. In recent times we have witnessed the example of a church which calls itself Christian refusing to accept non-white Christians as members. There are numerous examples wherein a Christian church has been impelled to request one of its members, who had "sinned heavily," to depart from its congregation.

For the church this problem has been there from the beginning. When Paul began formulating the discipline for organized Christianity, he was required to compromise some of the ideals of the faith. Primitive Christianity, raw and uncut, is an idyllic philosophy for a life, but it always has been a mighty poor basis for an organization. One must recognize, therefore, that a Christian church is conceived out of paradox and should not be painted with blame simply because its acts are not in every respect consistent with the teachings of Christ. Recently this writer heard a lady steadfastly defend a national policy which required that the United States Air Force bomb the territory of another nation. Said she, "This is a Christian nation, and we intend to keep it that way." There were a number present, and all seemed to understand exactly what she meant.

---

[10] Edward Gibbon, *The Decline and Fall of the Roman Empire* (Philadelphia: Claxton, Remsen, and Haffelfinger, 1880), Volume II, p. 84.

In the Gospel according to St. Matthew, Christ spoke to Peter and the disciples saying, "Thou art Peter, and on this rock I will build my church and the gates of hell shall not prevail against it and I will give you the keys to the kingdom of heaven . . ."[11] According to tradition, Peter did found the church, but before he did, on the eve of the crucifixion, as Jesus foretold he would, Peter experienced the paradox of Christianity. He denied Christ three times. Peter had to do this in order to go on being Peter and to establish the church. We can take this as evidence that Christ understood the paradox and the conflicts it would thrust upon those who found life through Him and yet had to go on living in a world that knew Him not. The founder of the church experienced paradox, and churches have experienced it ever since.

Because of the paradox it is possible for us to reason that a church in the sense that it is an organization can not be Christian. Some come a great deal closer to being Christian than others, but the paradox is always there. In this reasoning, therefore, *only a man can be Christian.* What does an organized Christian church do? It makes Christianity possible in men. Whatever else the church may claim to be, it is primarily a teacher. It must fight the battles it fights in order that it can teach Christ to men who wish to be Christian. By this we also understand that the *church is not a religion* nor can a church *establish a religion.* A religion can only be established by a man, and he can establish it only in one place. That place *is in himself.* Religion in man is established man by man, each choosing his own.

The Christian church, if it functions as it ought, sustains the possibility that Christianity can come alive in men. The "keys to the kingdom" can be thought of as keys to the inner life and after life of ecstacy and love. A child who is becoming a Christian or a Jew or an atheist is becoming what he is becoming while on public as well as on private property. For reasons we have shown and continue to show it is mainly the becoming Christian whose needs are unmet in the current modes of public education. The others are cared for more adequately.

Let us picture what would occur if a church were invited into a public school building at the request of the family and community to help those becoming Christians with prayer and related meditation; we can feel assured that legal action would intervene. The church would be forbidden this teaching function in the public school on the

---

[11] Matthew 16:18-19.

legal grounds that Congress cannot establish a religion. This result would ensure despite our argument that it is not the Congress, not the church, but the child who is establishing the religion, and he is establishing it only in himself. The church can help but nowise can do the job, and Congress could not establish a religion even if it tried. Continuing the illustration, the church is now barred from the school, but the child remains. He is still establishing the religion of his life and he is doing so in an environment in which non-church or anti-church religious influences predominate.

Many will disagree with this argument, but more than a few will sense its substance and emerge with the feeling that we cannot stop with court decrees. Men do not live by laws alone; sooner or later they become philosophic about what happens to them. They then apply the metacriteria. They make the move to higher ground. They see that judges become tangled in tentacles of language, precedent, and statute, and the view from the bench may not be clear. This view can not see religion as other than a problem of institutions, of laws. But in reality a religious problem is a child growing up, encountering life, forming values, developing insight, and coming to feel how it is to be an American.

We Will Come Rejoicing

A central concern in any study of theism is the nature of man's fellowship with God.[12] Of special interest here is the aesthetic dimension. There is beauty about it; there is beauty in it. Man's sense of beauty is interlocked with his sense of God in that central life passion which earlier in these pages was called man's religious nature. There is great beauty in modern expressions of theism. Much of the art of Western culture has been inspired by these expressions; and this art, in turn, has served to intensify their inherent beauty. In a religious sense joy is beauty in belief. The ubiquitous presence of beauty in man's fellowship with God makes it possible for a theist to rejoice in his personal religion.

Judaism is a beautiful religion. It is the oldest of the major Western religions. The solemn grace of its ceremonies, rites, and customs, and the incomparable splendor of Hebrew letters have enabled Judaism to sustain an unbroken power over the prospectives of its adherents for more than four thousand years. It originated among the nomadic

---

[12] Harry Emerson Fosdick, *A Guide to Understanding the Bible* (New York: Harper and Brothers, 1938), p. 201-256.

herdsmen who traveled the fertile crescent which was anchored on one side by the Valley of the Nile and on the other side by the Tigris and Euphrates rivers. Its people were in Egypt for nearly four centuries. In the final years of this period they were out of favor, victims of an oppressive bondage. The sojourn in the barren wilderness of the Sinai Peninsula exceeded forty years. These were the years they grew strong and unified under great leaders. Their conquests of the Valley of the Jordan occupied the better part of a century. The Israelites then rose to nationhood and, on the power of the sword, became the sovereign of their neighbors. Then came civil war, decline, conquest, and exile. Provincial or commonwealth status existed for a time, but in 70 A.D., following the sack of Jerusalem by the Emperor Titus, the Jews dispersed throughout the world. Later, after the Middle Ages, the virus of anti-semitism afflicted Europe and the Middle East and for a thousand years the Jew was hounded, scorned, and persecuted, but he survived. In recent times the Jew has regained a national home. At the same time, there are indications that man's thousand-year virus may be nearing its end.

It was not a beautiful religion in the beginning. In the days of the patriarchs it was a brutal thing which fostered such abominations as human sacrifice, torture, and disfigurement. The evidence on this is pitifully clear. "Yahweh spake unto Moses, saying, Sanctify unto me all the first born, whatsoever openeth the womb among the children of Israel, both of man and of beast; it is mine."[13] The tradition lasted a long time even though terminated in legend by the experience of Abraham and Isaac. One can not fail to be moved by the vision of Abraham leading his son to the site of sanctification. What inner torment this would cause in any man whose religious passions were summoned for the suppression of his paternal passions. Yet, in what must have been an hour of unsurpassed agony, he did not turn his face from God. Isaac was redeemed and the time came when animals replaced man at the sacrificial altar. Even in this way the hideous business continued and the temples with their bloody and smoking altars remained shrines to a God who demanded constant appeasement. The priests, the Levites, nourished this fear and unapproachableness.[14]

But time wore on and the wild, turbulent temple scenes were reformed and sublimed into ceremonies of sacrament and consecration. The Jewish family, always defined by the beloved law, was inte-

---

[13] Exodus 13:1-2.
[14] Exodus 19:21-22.

grated into the observances. Judaism began to mature. The Messianic vision of the prophets gave it the leaven of hope of fulfillment. This quality of sanguine expectation has not been lost and the twin senses of identity and of destiny which it has perpetuated gives the Jew a perspective of himself and a purpose to his life which some other religious traditions withhold.

The aesthetic experience of Judaism is that of feeling the heartbeat of a religion which has been pulsing in men for forty centuries. The vivid symbols and the acts to which they are connected bring the celebrant into a passionate connection with his past and future. It enrolls him in a family of men who have a special purpose in going on with the matter of being what they are. All of it revolves around the great tradition of letters and a pathos for mankind which is felt in the deep and secret places of human experience. To those capable of steadfastness and resolve in the authentic heritage of the Jew the thing becomes immensely beautiful. The God of the Jew is both personal and approachable through prayer. When the beauty of his fellowship with God is merged with the aesthetic qualities of his religious tradition, the Jew has the experience of joy in his life.

Christianity, too, is a beautiful religion. The aesthetic dimensions of Christianity tend more to be expressed in personification and in painting, sculpture, music, and architecture. It also has a profound literary tradition, but it is not equal to Hebrew letters. Only two of the four gospels and the letters of Paul appear of the same quality range as the Books of the Old Testament. The early disciples of Christianity were plain men who worked with their hands. They were ablaze with a new idea and living in the expectation that the end of things was imminent and the Kingdom of God was at hand. Moreover, they were more concerned with the spiritual inwardness of God; they wanted to feel Him more than to understand His concrete nature. Nearly eight centuries were to pass before Christians began to develop a strong literary tradition.

Christianity is ever to be at odds with the critical or realistic historian. Christ is not a historical figure. As Santayana points out, "The Christ men have loved and adored is an ideal of their own hearts, the construction of an ever present personality, living and intimately understood, out of the fragments of story and doctrine connected with a name." There are a great many things, Christian and non-Christian, which are powerful influences in human values which have no reality in the standards of historical realism. The Virgin Mary is a great influence in Christian thought. She offers even a clearer example of this "inward building of an ideal form." The idea contains two aesthetic qualities, the first is purity and the second is universal motherhood. Together they create a standard of perfection in womanhood which has inspired and dominated the Christian imagination. It is not merely metaphysics made comprehensible to the common man, it is an experience in ideality which is as real as human feeling is real.[15]

The cross and the Mother have served as themes for countless works of art. The wine and the wafer are also symbols of formal Christian ideas. Although Christians dispute whether their significance is material or allegorical, they are nevertheless gratifying in their beauty. The communion service is meant in part to be an experience in the beauty of these forms. Christian music ranges from the convulsive symmetry of Bach and Handel to the warm but dynamic simplicity of the Protestant hymns. Musical forms of Christian ideas mean a great deal to the Christian. He is not being informed about God in the critical or realistic sense. Instead he is experiencing God in his inner will, and the effects are beautiful. But these symbols and forms are not essential to the Christian life any more than the church itself is essential. However one arrives at a Christian life does not change the proposition that *Christianity is only real when it is in life.* It is seen only in the attitudes which are held toward God and the things of the world.

Although aesthetic experience in the literary arts, graphic arts, music, and prayer are not essential to either Judaism or Christianity, those who are interested in the development of values will be quick to assert that the religious experience which grows upon a fellowship with God is greatly intensified by the presence of and expressions of beauty.

The man who has learned to sense beauty has the capacity to open every aspect of his being and fill it more fully with life. Everything he experiences is better experience for his having a sense of beauty. This applies to his religious nature which, as has been said, is the fundamental aspect of being. As the pure scientist finds beauty in science, the pure Christian finds beauty in life.

Christians and Jews have tended to work against rather than for each other in maintaining the aesthetic dimensions of their respective traditions in the school environment. Christians, of course, are the

---

[15] George Santayana, *The Sense of Beauty* (New York: Dover Publications Inc., 1955), p. 189.

majority group in America. Their religious expressions are more visible because they range the art forms more widely. The Jew who does not understand this, and resents it, raises his voice against the music and the art. He may not realize that the Christian depends on these expressions to the same general extent that the Jew depends upon law and tradition. It is highly doubtful if Christian religious forms and symbols in and of themselves convert Jewish children. Once a Jewish girl sang in a school chorus performance of Handel's *Messiah*. During the performance there were tears in her eyes. When it ended she exclaimed, "It is so beautiful." This girl was no less Jewish for this experience; if anything, her religious nature was intensified. The words meant nothing; the aesthetic experience was all. If anything, she was more Jewish than before.

Theists of all traditions have served their beliefs badly by working against each other. The suppression of religious art and prayer in school has spurred the predominance of antitheistic and atheistic influences. Is this what is wanted? Wanted or not, it is occurring. Children have an appetite for beauty. There is much beauty in the world not associated with theism. So a man can rejoice in his beliefs whether they are for or against God.

On the other hand, a mature people can not only abide the visibility of religious expressions other than their own; they can be enriched by them. This writer has been deeply impressed by parents of children in the Lehigh University Laboratory School. Out of necessity, this school has had to rent space in the Bethlehem Jewish Community Center and the Lutheran Church. Both buildings contain numerous forms and symbols. There are Jewish parents who have children in the classrooms of the Church and, of course, Christian parents bring their children to the Center which has thoughtfully suspended kosher requirements on the lunches these children bring. It is in this largeness and liberality of spirit that Americans can find better approaches to this problem.

It is appropriate again to quote Gibbon who made this observation of the attitudes the Romans had toward religion in the years of their ascendancy before the elements of decline took effect:

> The various modes of worship, which prevailed in the Roman world, were all considered by the people as equally true; by the philosophers as equally false; and by the magistrate as

equally useful. And thus tolerance produced not only mutual indulgence, but even religious concord.[16]

An attitude of this kind appears appropriate for the future of religious pluralism. Let us have our religions out in the open so all can help each rejoice in his own.

The Public Choice

Speculation is in order. The problem is vastly complicated by serious obstacles in two areas. One, of course, is the requirement that freedom and tolerance be given more than an abstract reality. Like religion itself, these things do not exist except in the attitudes of people. The second obstacle is in the form of needed legal and administrative reforms. If the two obstacles are removed the way will open to assure that traditional theism will remain a possible religious choice for the Americans of the future.

It is not necessary to elaborate further on the problems of freedom and tolerance beyond saying that they are seldom realized national ideals to be enjoyed by both *majority* and *minority* groups and no general solution is possible in the field of religious education unless they are really actualized in the attitudes of people. Given this, then sensible legal and administrative reforms have a prospect of success. Foremost among the needed reforms is an amendment which will exempt public schools from the recent interpretations of the first amendment. As it now stands, there is nothing a school can do except teach courses *about* religion. This will not produce religiousness; in fact, such courses are expressly designed to avoid this. The required administrative reform is the establishment of *authentic* local control of public education with particular reference to any aspect of the curriculum which deals with religious experience. This latter idea is highly instrumental and does require elaboration.

For a variety of reasons, none without merit, state and national authority has combined to reduce local control of public education. Among some national leaders there appears to be a propensity to mistrust local responsibility. The belief is clear that American communities are not to be trusted with the tax money returned to them for the work of education. It must be used as the federal government directs. Moreover, educational conversation on education reveals a pervasive notion that every solution must be a national solution. We

---

[16] Gibbon, *op. cit.*, Volume I, p. 34.

have been taking public schools away from the people. To deal with the problem of religious education the public will have to insist that local control be restored.

Public schools won public acceptance on the wings of local control. Naturally, every community did not do what every other community did. But instead of one national solution or one state solution there were thousands of local solutions which were worked out by local communities. And why should this not be? The strength of the nation is in its towns and neighborhoods. Everywhere we are weakening the fabric of local school districts by administrative designs which deter local leadership from acting on local problems. It will not be an easy thing for big government to untie the strings. Big combinations have formed which have a vested interest in big support and big control. However, there is no conceivable way that big government can deal with the matter of religious experience for children. This again is a case where thousands of local solutions must be found in every place where men and women enjoy the life-fulfilling experience of watching their children grow and of sharing in the decisions which affect their education.

The federal government is not omnipresent nor is it omniscient. As for morality, there is good reason to doubt that Washington is more moral than Center Valley. The problems are severe enough at the local level; it would be wildly absurd to seek macrocosmic solutions. If big government can mount the wisdom to allow local solutions to develop and the tolerance to accept even what it does not like, public education might well be redeemed.

There are three alternatives which local communities could accept. The first of the three involves giving parents credit in a public account which can be used to send the children to a private school of their own choosing. The second alternative which becomes possible under the administrative reform urged here is that local authority be empowered to work out solutions within the existing framework of public education. The third alternative of the three is to do nothing. This would result in the reduction of theism to a relic of the past, to be an historic interest along with the polytheism of pagan antiquity. The public will choose one of these three and possibly modify it with variations of the other two.

The first alternative envisions a return to private education as the principal educational enterprise in America. In this conception the role of government becomes inspectional and, to some extent, standard setting. There is something to be said for this. Although the public schools have been magnificent in most respects, it will have to be admitted that they have become large, impersonal, and, to an increasing extent, they are bureaucratic. Much "consolidation" was accomplished in pursuit of values which were examined in haste, accepted with reservation, and reviewed with regret. The public schools have been undersupported at local levels; they have not solved their own teacher shortage, and public confidence in certain areas has faded dangerously. Now they are beset by teacher strikes, a form of rancor destructive of any educational environment. There is a growing tendency to by-pass the schools in dealing with new educational problems. A resurgence of private effort could have a salutory effect all the way around.

But a return to private education on a massive scale presents even bigger problems. The magnitude of modern education makes private education an impossible alternative. Private schools are non-profit (in fact, they invariably require support beyond tuition). Funding is hard to come by. The advisability of "donating" or allocating public funds in the amounts required is to be seriously questioned. Moreover, the unity of the people could be seriously shattered by the fragmentation which would ensue. Private education has problems of its own.

Even though public schools have difficulty with religious education, and are confronted with a host of vexations, they are established and have demonstrated their potential. In each community there are school buildings at various stages of being paid for. Parents send their children there willingly and, in many cases, proudly. More than a few public schools are equal to or better than the best private schools. These have proved what can be done. In perspective, the public schools are an heroic achievement, unique to America. It seems obvious the better answer is in the further development.

This brings forth the second alternative. It proposes a truly local public school which has the freedom to act in response to the attitudes of its community. The present role of a local school board has been reduced to battling professional employees and various community interests within a narrow and increasingly rigid framework of policy. This alternative reposes faith in the idea that a clever, industrious, imaginative, and innovative people will find solutions to problems if they have freedom to act.

Recently a government official is reported to have remarked that federal money was not going to various parts of the country in the "pious hope" that it would be wisely used. The speaker meant to disparage no one, and his meaning was understood. However, it must not escape notice that the American people, going about local business in local ways, have produced the unprecedented wealth upon which the federal budget has been raised. No one would deny that some direction or control by government officials is needed, but placing resources in the hands of responsible Americans at the community level has got to be more than a pious hope. If it isn't, there is no hope at all.

If the legal barriers to theistic expression in public schools are brought down, community solutions will emerge. Arguments by anti-theists and atheists that this violates their freedoms or rights are philosophically indefensible and morally abominable. Atheists who advance such views (and most of them don't) should educate themselves on their own religious nature in order that they can see how their injunctions work to foster their creed upon others. Because most atheists are also people of high integrity they will probably recant and allow others the freedom they demand for themselves.

The third alternative is to do nothing. This would produce one of two possible effects. The first and least likely of the two is a revitalization of Christian church and family. However, many modern social and economic considerations are working against this. The school and college environment is more dominant now, and it will probably become even more so. Therefore, the second and most probable effect will prevail if the school and college environments continue partial to antitheistic and atheistic religions; the second effect being that subsequent generations will be increasingly disinclined to join and support the church. The religious needs of our people will be filled by the secular religions of the school. And we can anticipate the churches will become "tombs and sepulchers of God" as Nietzsche prophesied.

Judaism will last longer. Here family, law, and tradition are strong influences, but time will also run out for the American Jew. The hardy traditions which withstood forty centuries of time, trial, dispersion, and persecution may not survive the growing indifferences of on-coming generations whose religious needs are met in other ways and places.

The Brave New School

Let us imagine what a local community might do if it had the legal freedom and administrative authority to work out its own solutions to the religious development of the youth. First of all, religious and educational leaders, both lay and professional, would have reason to come together and *reason*. One would hope that the great churches which have centralized authority would enter into this spirit of localism by allocating to local clergy broad power in negotiation. The centralized church could go even further by emphasizing to such local leaders that it expects them to deal creatively with the opportunities inherent in such local discussion.

There would be moments of trial and despair. In every community, feelings have been long "bottled up." Once released they will take the forms of rancor and discord. But leadership should emerge, "statesmanship" should prevail, and issues should resolve. This ecumenical hope could not have been so much as a dream thirty years ago. However, a great deal has happened. We know much more, attitudes have changed, and the reasons for concord have never been more compelling. These factors can be counted upon to join with the same good American common sense which a century ago brought neighbors to the aid of a burned-out farmer, and produced other prodigies of cooperation which are fondly recalled in even this competitive era with its formal aloofness and stylish detachment.

A community which forms a successful protocol for religious experience in its public schools would *soon* become a model to be respected and followed. The word "soon" is not to be taken as a matter of months. Such developments require more time than this. What is the cadence by which traditions grow? The chronometrics of man offer a choice which begins with microseconds and extends to millenia. Changes of the sort described here require between ten and fifty years, depending on the strength of the factors which urge them on and the tenacity of the factors that hold them back. The perspective of history will have to be brought to the gauge of progress. Impatience can be as vigorous an enemy of progress as open resistance.

The brave new school of this vision is the opposite of that which might belong in Huxley's *Brave New World*. For example, a community could agree that Christian personifications, art, and music could remain visible to all children. Their meaning to atheist and Jewish children is allegorical and not historical. The same could be said of many, if not most, Christian children who have come to view them as representations of indwelling ideals. Their visibility would enrich the religious nature of all children regardless of the creed to which the family is connected. Likewise, Jewish holidays and customs can be respected in public policy. More public notice should be taken of the great Jewish traditions. Jewish families should be pleased to share with others the sense of the past and the sense of destiny so implicit in the Torah. No American Christian could fail to be strengthened in his life by a fuller understanding of the very remarkable people who have been their neighbors but too often have been forced to remain strangers. Both Christian and Jew are poorer because of this strangeness.

Atheistic children, too, must be respected. Teachers and school officials could educate themselves and the children to understand that atheism must be respected as another religion. No atheist is without moral foundations for his life. This foundation, and not whether he does or does not include God in his personal metaphysics, must be our basis for valuing him as a human being. The atheist can learn tolerance along with the believers in other religious forms.

In this school, time and space can be set aside for Christian children to engage in the prayer and meditation so important in both the developing and the mature Christian. His fellowship with God may require prayer more than other God-centered religions which establish the fellowship on other bases. This can be respected; it offends no one; if provided and supervised in the proper spirit, it will put a dimension in the school environment which will benefit all.

Modern writers tend to view Utopias with dismay. The Utopias of Orwell and Huxley are horrifying. This brave new school need horrify no one except those who are inclined to impress a distressing sameness upon every public school. This Utopia is based on three faiths: (1) a faith in tolerance, (2) a faith in freedom, and (3) a faith that in diversity there is a profound and continuing strength. All this calls upon us to do is to accept in our practical life the precepts which have been on our lips for many, many years.

Will there be perfect harmony? At rare times, yes; at most times, no. Tolerance, freedom, and diversity tend to produce social abrasions. These, however, heal quickly and a healthy society lives on. But a society of men whose religious vision is deprived of the beauty of symbol and idiom which is embedded in the theistic religions of our Western heritage and deprived of the indwelling ideals which these religions have fostered will be ill-suited for the rigors of tomorrow. The crisis of values which is emerging in American life can not be resolved by men suddenly impoverished of that which has for long been their greatest source of strength. To put it simply, we must all stand taller and conclude the long warfare which has kept the theistic religious creeds from establishing a basis for their own survival.

CHAPTER VII

The Examined Life and the Crisis in Values

At life's first breath black sails are stretched
   For death erewhile on course
The meaning of the voyage is etched
   By values grown in force.
We seek not ends which are forlorn
   Grief is by life imposed
But thorns of being are best forborne
   When in beauty enclosed.

DIALOGUE

Student: The older generation complains constantly about the values of the younger. They say a crisis of values is developing. Why do they do this? Are there not always problems between the young and the old? Have not the young always done new things which the old dislike, and do not the old always wish the young would continue being as they were?

Teacher: You have a strong point, but do you not think that any civilization is under the necessity and stress of sustaining itself and growing stronger, and in these days of rapid change do you not think the problem of sustaining and strengthening is unique?

Student: Certainly no more so than many occasions long past. It was a conservative generation which murdered Socrates because he was the friend of the young generation and encouraged them to think their own thoughts rather than the thoughts of their fathers. We are told that this was a time of rapid change in Athens. Are we also to martyr a modern spokesman for change?

Teacher: The charge against Socrates was more complicated than that. But you are right in part; one thing we can learn from this is that civilizations do not sustain themselves simply by fortifying their gods.

Student: By this do we learn that a civilization lives on by killing its obsolete gods and bringing on new gods as the new need arises?

Teacher: Some men say this, but I fear we speak of different things and are confounded by the difference. By gods you refer to ideals that men hold and to which they give names such as Venus, who might be an ideal of love and beauty in women; Mercury, who is the ideal of the gymnast in men; Bacchus, who might be the ideal of perfection in wine;

Pan, who could be called the ideal of responsibility in shepherds; and each of the Muses who represents ideals in various arts and histories. But a polytheism of this kind implies a pluraverse or polyverse.

Student: And we live in a universe?

Teacher: The word universe implies that all things turn in one. This is not so much an ideal as it is a view of reality, and it is a view of reality that is theologically consistent with a single God. The origins of monotheism are buried in antiquity but the notion of a universe dates from the teachings of Thales, Anaximander, and Heraclitus.

Student: Then monotheism is consistent with traditional philosophy and polytheism is not?

Teacher: Yes. Except for formal Platonism. Plato tended to enshrine separate ideals. But Aristotle seemed to unify them in his principle of actuality.

Student: But what of modern philosophy? Does not pragmatism reteach pluralism? Does pragmatism also give society freedom to make its own ideals and deify them?

Teacher: Pragmatism teaches that society forms ideals but it prefers that no deities be formed. Pragmatism teaches that ideals constantly change; making ideals into gods would slow the change and cause violence.

Student: Should we call pragmatism a kind of convertible or streamlined polytheism?

Teacher: That would be stretching it much too far, but you have developed the idea that pragmatism is inconsistent with monotheism. Some pragmatists seem to want to deify change itself, and in their religious nature they are devoted to the processes of change. We call them methodological atheists, but they are very religious about their methodology.

Student: Both traditional and modern philosophy, as well as all religious creeds, admit to the existence of ideals but differ as to their origin, permanence, and manner of expression?

Teacher: To know what is good a man must discover what he holds most dear. You have discovered that men seek ideals in different ways. You have also found that the health of civilization is somehow reflected in the change or lack of change of these ideals. You have also found that ideals associated with deity are slower to change and this may be good or bad for the health of the civilization. But your first question was about the crisis of values. What have you discovered about this?

Student: I have discovered that it would be a good thing to know which ideals build or sustain a civilization and which ideals tear it down. I have also discovered this is of especial concern in a time of rapid change.

Teacher: What about the religious creeds which relate to those values?

Student: It seems to me that theists, pantheists, and atheists can unify on the grounds that civilization should go on and become stronger if that is possible. Men of all creeds should deliberate together on the problems of ideality and ideology. Their separate religious natures may result in differences, but these can be resolved in rational dialectic.

Teacher: Are you saying that all men should examine the ideals to which their civilization is holding, or to which it should be aspiring, regardless of their belief or non-belief in God?

Student: One aspect of an ideal life is that it should be an examined life. Belief or non-belief in God deals more with *how* a man looks at life. Believing in God does not require the believer to stop his mind from thinking or require that he listen only to priests.

Teacher: Is this not what Socrates really said? After all, he was not simply for the young and against the old. He really wanted all men to look carefully at their ideals and to understand their meaning. He also thought God wanted men to do this.

Student: Now that you have said what you have said, I recall that his prosecutors proposed that he stop teaching, stop his relentless questioning, stop his tricking men into doubt about what they do and say. But he responded that they really wanted him to stop examining life and he indicated that an unexamined life was not worth living. This being the case, he cheerfully took the poison.

Teacher: I like your analysis of the matter. If I am correct, you now think the crisis of values in Athens was in the failure of men to examine ideals during a time of rapid change.

Student: Yes, not long after Socrates died, the elements of decline in Athenian civilization became clear. It was evident by their nature that these same elements had been forming for many years.

Teacher: But Socrates had many distinguished students who became distinguished philosophers and started great schools. These students wept at his martyrdom and some of them devoted their lives to philosophy, giving it that tradition of rigor which we call Socratic.

Student: His students wept, and they teach us. But the heart of Athens was not moved by Socrates or his students. Did not Aristophanes mock them? The downward course of Athens was unchecked by all that Socrates said and did.

Teacher: Then the words of Socrates are for us and were not for the Athenians?

Student: Yes, he gave us the first ideal upon which to build and sustain a civilization.

Teacher: What is that?

Student: Certainly the ideal life must be an examined life.

Teacher: This is not an argument against any religious creed?

Student: No, in fact, it is an argument for all of them because each can make its own contribution to the resolution of the modern crisis in values, because each represents a mode of life examination. All religions are precious.

Teacher: Then we have a crisis?

Student: I think we do, because our ideals are not adequately examined in a time of rapid change.

POLEMIC

We are falling! But we cannot feel the fall; our reflexes are deadened by the sweet poisons of wealth and luxury. See how our institutions fade! Their tissue and bone are dissolved in the septic waters of change and indifference. What madness it is to put them in greater buildings, express them in lavish ceremonies, and compose words in praise of them to be bound up in beautiful books. If institutions exist not in the ideals of men, then they are nowhere. When men cease to love their country, their country ceases. When men cease to revere their God, their God is dead. When men cease to respect their homes, their homes vanish. When men cease to idealize woman, woman vanishes and in her place stands a craving animal.

How can we help ourselves? What is there that will save us from the fate of Alexandria, Israel, Babylon, Athens, Rome, and the great cities of the Renaissance? Are we destined to repeat the same cycle? Institutions live in the societies of men but have their birth, their life, and their death in the mind and spirit of man. We call them institutions when they are outside of man doing their work in the raw world of senses. Inside of men they are called ideals. There are two ways an institution can vanish. It vanishes when the ideal it expresses vanishes in man; it vanishes when it separates itself from the continuing ideal.

The ideals which made the great institutions by which our civilization is known have begun to diminish. The institutions which express those dying ideals go on for a while, making prodigious heaves, creating the illusion of vigor and health. But they are dying; the vertebrate connection has been severed and we see only the reflex action of a dying creature, which lives yet a while; yet it is dead, irreversibly dead.

We move about in the shells of dead and dying institutions. They are dying because of the prior death of ideality. Institutions of education, the family, the church, the school nourish ideals. These allowed ideality to fade and the decline began; the decline fed upon healthy tissue and increased itself. It has become a malignancy!

What hand held the blade which plunged into the core of our vitality?
It was the philosophy of process! Never mind your external goals,
it sweetly sang. Education merely reconstructs the experience of man!
The goals of mankind are myths; the goals of society are real! Bring
your eyes down from the Olympian crest and dwell upon your social
wants and needs. Here is all the truth that ever was and all you'll
ever know. Wash away the pain of aspiration and master the processes
which bring you comfort. What compassion we can have for the
dirty and poor of other lands so long as our processes keep us the
masters of material!

There is power in information. Men who acquire information can
join this power with other powers inherent in their creature wants
and needs, and the world becomes their plaything. They can dirty
its skies, pollute its waters, poison its creatures, ravage its minerals,
and waste its soils. They leave it to their sons a little worse than they
found it. Their responsibility is to the shekel and not to the earth. But
the earth has its victory in their grave.

Oh, men of the city! You pile stone and glass high above the
streets. Your women burlesque womanhood and you burlesque your
manhood. You go into your theaters which mock "main street" and
the oafishness of the unlettered, and your laughter is heard in the
streets. Your tolerance is great, but it comes not from generosity; your
tolerance is derived from your indifference. You rise in lofty towers
and marvel at the view of ugly roof tops. What manner of creatures are
you? How do you remind yourselves that you are men? Look at the
shelves of your bookstores! You gamble, you kill, you take drugs,
you watch pugilists at work, you are ruthless in competition, and the
trauma of sex constantly absorbs your minds. This is the savagery by
which you achieve feeling. Men who live as you do cannot feel in
other ways.

You print the books and fashion the entertainment for the people
of the towns and villages. You have led the way in breaking their
ideals. You use these ideals for your own purposes, and in your hands
they become dust and ashes. Commerce is your god. Your other gods
work for commerce.

How can our fall be stopped? We must rekindle human feeling!
We must redeem our ideals so that they can once again warm our
imagination, can teach us of the good, and can make us heroes. We
must teach our children the knowledge of feeling as well as the knowledge of information. They must feel the hard reality of the abstract
nouns. We cannot take the man out of the city, but we can take the

city out of the man. He can be taught to sense the beauty of ideals and in their abstract representations expressions of the religious creeds. Man can put his own beauty into the city and drive out its savagery.

Oh, the children of the ghetto! First give them beauty, then give them skill. The poverty of their lives is the absence of inspiration and ideality. Without this inspiration their skills are without purpose, and their lives are without direction. We must first minister to their being and then attend to their doing. Several wise men have said that we learn to do by doing. But we also learn to be by being, and what kind of being have we given to the children of the ghetto? First give them beauty; without beauty reason founders, and skills become the tricks of clever devils.

The restoration of ideals will produce restoration in the life institutions. But all must begin at the places where children learn. It is not great wealth that is needed here. We must restore to these environments the kind of teacher who can bring children to feats of abstraction in the ideal order. This involves a style of teaching which inevitably confronts the religious nature of every child who is becoming what he can become. What a great act of courage it will require for our nation to admit that religiousness and right education are one and inseparable.

DISCOURSE

The Crisis in Values

Values have always created abrasive relationships between generations. The literature of both Biblical and pagan antiquity reflect the anxieties of those times about the attitudes and excesses of the youth. One might suppose there has always been something of a crisis in values. The verdict of the Athenian jury which martyred Socrates was in part a species of discontent with attitudes of the young whose rebellious propensities were encouraged by the Athenian sage. The fact that irritation over values is not new does not alter the intensity of feelings about it. The adult generation always has good reason to struggle for continuity, and there are very good reasons to think that the struggle of the modern adult generation is both unique and difficult.

The reason for the uniqueness of our contemporary struggle is that never before have the consequences of regression been so severe. It is usually conceded that the development of civilization has not been ever upward. There were recognized lapses, some of them colossal. However, in the past, men were somewhat limited in the damage they could inflict upon themselves and each other. Now that man's capacity for mischief is infinite, it is correct to think that men have lost forever the privilege of being irresponsible. The bridges back to barbarism have burned away. We could never make it back alive. This circumstance alone makes the present crisis more unique than any before.

In several ways it is more difficult. One of the difficulties is reflected in the loss of the certainty in values which was characteristic of preceding generations. If parents and teachers of today are asked what values should be preserved, or are worth preserving, the answers would be ringed by doubt and qualification. We have seen so much change. A single generation has broken so many former barriers in physics and technology that past notions about the cosmos and man's relationship to it have been shattered; new ones are forming but forming very slowly. Thus, it goes far beyond fashions in dress, sexual promiscuity, styles in dancing, and customs in marriage. The most general statement which can be made is that fundamental changes are occurring in the personal metaphysics of man and we have not begun to understand the nature of the changes.

It is unfortunate, therefore, that we have separated metaphysics from the classroom and religion from education.[1] The time has come again for man to reflect deeply on his nature. Time is now measured in microseconds and distance in light years. Theistic ideas of God have been giving ground to pantheistic and atheistic ideas. More and more we are believing other things about the nature of God. Our views on freedom have become almost inverted. At one time we spoke of freedom *for* work, freedom *for* worship, and freedom *for* opportunity. Now the idea of freedom is freedom *from* things, and we speak of freedom *from* fear, freedom *from* hunger, and freedom *from* want.

Another radical change in personal metaphysics relates to the matter of constancy. Our parents tended to say that fundamental reality was constant and unchanged, fixed and dependable. They spelled their truth with a capital "T." It was absolute. Today, students of educational philosophy are encouraged to think that reality is a changing thing. There are many realities because reality is situational. There is a changing truth in each situation and this truth is spelled with a small "t." Of truth we can say there is none except that it is true that everything is in process of becoming something else. Involution, evolution, and revolution[2] are constant and forever. We have come again to the view of Heraclitus, the ancient sage of Ephesus, "You cannot step twice in the same river for yet other waters are constantly flowing on to you."[3]

We would no longer accredit those moving phrases which introduce our Declaration of Independence. We no longer accept self-evident truth and self-evident knowledge. Now all knowledge except the knowledge of pure mathematics requires empirical verification, experimental proof, or must be instrumental. Formerly, we accepted reason and authority; today our standard is sense perception. At one time logic was mainly induction and deduction. Modern logic gives more weight to dialectic. Ethics has moved from perfectionism to utilitarianism and more recently toward hedonism. No examination

---

[1] Richard Weaver, *Ideas Have Consequences* (Chicago: University of Chicago Press, Phoenix Edition, 1965), pp. 148-69.

[2] Keyser, *op. cit.*

[3] Fragments 41-42.

of metaphysics can produce an undisputed judgment of bad or good. We can, however, see that there is change, massive change. With this instability in the personal metaphysics of the adult generation one can not expect hard or firm lines to be drawn on value issues. In fact, many adults under the urging of mental hygienists have taken to asking panels of children what values should be held. All of this adds up to uncertainty and this makes the contemporary value struggle more difficult.

Another difficulty alluded to earlier[4] is inherent in the style of scholarship in philosophy and education. We have become primarily oriented to process. In educational philosophy this orientation reached its highest expression in John Dewey, and perhaps its most straightforward application to educational practice was presented by William Kilpatrick. Such an orientation openly shuns *a priori* goals for life and extra-natural standards for value. Men are not understood as beings of special creation. Men are social and vocal phenomena who have reality only in the processes of the society with which they are identified. That society forms the ideals through a function of group mind called "consensus." Matters of taste and sentiment are determined by the collective mind of the group or public. Society becomes the sole arbiter of the good. Public ideals are achieved by open inquiry and discourse. Public feelings about ideals are made known by the various ways the public expresses itself.

An entertainer can be good television one year, but may be bad television the next year. In a decade, the public judgment about gambling may change it from a bad thing to a good thing. Some time ago we were forbidden to play games of a certain kind on the Sabbath. Now, the Sabbath is only Sunday. It is a splendid time for baseball, tennis, bowling, or movies. The mystique of public consensus changes bad to good and good to bad. There is no "hitching post" for value, nothing permanent, nothing enduring.

Traditional philosophy was inclined to behave as if it had permanent truth locked somewhere in the closet. A good enough philosopher could rummage around, find it, and get it out for those who asked it of him. Modern philosophers do not work with this kind of illusion (although they may have their own). They are interested in how we think, what we think, how we know, what we know, and how we make meaning of our words. Permanence, invariance have no place in this pragmatic, tough-minded Twentieth Century. Our era

---

[4] See Chapter I.

belongs to the problem staters and solution seekers. It belongs to the men whose truth is based upon successful experience in the ontology of process.

All of this is aggravated further by one more difficulty which must be reported. America views itself mainly through its channels of information and entertainment. We have the news publications, television, and motion pictures. Weaver[5] likened these to a great stereopticon. The machine is firmly under the control of those who manage it. All but a small fraction of the public are under its sway. They sit, as in a darkened room, and the pictures it makes for them constitute most of the reality they know. They impose upon it only three requirements: it must be easily available, it must be entertaining, it must be comprehensible. In exchange, a great portion of the public mind is handed over.

Lest this sound mildly paranoidal, it must be asserted the media managers have no conspiracy to control American thought. However, the media machine, by its nature, caters to the values inherent in bigness and in commerce. Small, independent newspapers are ceasing to be. Small, independent television networks never were. Men have criticized the view of reality spun out of these mass media. To hold attention with words and pictures it is often necessary to distort and dramatize. The limits of time and space require cutting, adapting, and selecting. There is a tendency to project an illusion objectively through journalistic stereotypes. Such stereotypes have laid a "dead hand of pattern" [6] upon the work of American journalists. Journalistic competition also creates an unfortunate need for sensation which has apparently forced even some reputable journalists to indicate that the "public right to know" is more precious than the privacy of any man about whom the public might have an exploitable curiosity.

Thus, in an era when truth on values is held by many to be deferential to a changing public mind, a great portion of that mind is entranced by a view of reality which is responsive to the values and interests of those who project it. It is impossible to know how much of the public mind is maneuvered, but one cannot avoid feeling

[5] Weaver, *op. cit.*, pp. 92-112.

[6] A phrase used by John Hay Whitney in an address at Colby College, Waterville, Maine, in 1964. Whitney was complaining that journalism had fallen in love with "a convention of objectivity that was to lay a dead hand of pattern on our news pages and freeze us into 'good form.'" (Although the reporter who writes "objectively" still selects the items of the story, and organizes the material, he attempts to preserve the illusion of objectivity in his style. The result is unreal and the authentic life of the story seldom emerges on the printed page.)

that much of it is maneuvered during this time when metaphysical beliefs are in transformation, education in traditional religious forms is in retreat, and man's capacity for self-destruction has reached the absolute. These combined factors make the present crisis in values both unique and difficult. Indeed, it is more unique and more difficult than any previous confrontation of its kind. In this way we establish the "crisis" as being more than an engaging phrase which, like so many others, is made only to catch the eye. The crisis is real, and the American people must come to sense its reality.

The Nature of the Ideal

How real is the ideal? Western philosophy has struggled with this question for more than 2,500 years. The answers vary within several traditions. Within the tradition called "formal idealism" Plato taught that ideals were absolutely real and that all else was an expression of them. In this system the ideal is independent of man who, nevertheless, has the power to know them abstractly and by this knowledge establish standards for the good. In the various traditions of realism the word "ideal" tends to disappear entirely in deference to operating principles by which essences are established. These principles, too, are independent of man, who, nevertheless, can discover them and use them to guide his quest for the good. Idealism depicts man as a thinking observer whereas realism changes the emphasis enough that he would be called an observing thinker. With the idealist, thought is the first probe for reality. The realist probes first by perception.

In the pragmatic tradition ideals have become goals which men or society conceive. As these goals may relate to men or their affairs, the goals are behavioral. Thus to the pragmatist the ideal is not independent of men. He wants to improve himself biologically and intellectually and constantly fashions higher goals for himself. In this way he knows the good, and he strives higher and higher as even higher goods are conceived. In the tradition of the existentialist all of this is put aside as each man is expected to contemplate his own particular existence and discover what this tells him about all else. His general goal is to fill out his existence as completely as he can. This involves discovering himself and the felicity and pain of choosing those beliefs, goals, or ideals which are most relevant to his existence.

This didactical interlude is intended merely to emphasize that no philosophical tradition which speaks at length about education has neglected the ideal in one form or another. One assigns to it the status of ultimate reality; another gives it only a contingent reality, but none of them withhold reality. Vital and meaningful as these distinctions are in academic philosophy they are not of moment to this discourse. The cardinal consideration here is that ideals are real and they have consequences.

A circle is an example of an ideal. It has never existed anywhere except in the mind. A circle can be approximated in material form. The approximation could be so great that a powerful microscope would be needed to discover the flaws, but the flaws are there. We know this because we know that man can not fully incarnate this ideal in his world of sensation. In the world of sensation, error is a universal constituent. Yet in the mind the ideal can remain pure and unalloyed. Once this ideal has been abstracted in the mind of a child he can discuss circles with others for the remainder of his life. The symbol "π" is used to identify the relationship between a radius and a circumference. If a value is given for one, the value of the other is axiomatic. The ideal of a circle has not changed since antiquity, and although more things may be discovered about it, it will not change so long as there is a mind to think of it.

Thus, it is correct to call a plate a plate, but it is incorrect to call it a circle. A circle can not exist in the world of sensation, but everywhere we look we see its consequences. Our eye falls continuously on wheels, gears, cylinders, and spheres. Without this ideal men would have very little of the present technology. Even though it is always about us it remains an *abstract noun*, something we can think but never perceive except in its approximated form.

The *abstract nouns* of geometry enjoy a clarity and stability that is withheld from others. Consider, for example, the abstract noun called "justice." Would that men could handle this ideal as easily as the circle. We can identify the approximation and applaud the draftsman's skill. Justice, on the other hand, rests upon a variety of metaphysical propositions. The ideal may have an *a priori* nature or it may be contingent. In either case we struggle for it constantly. Contrasting ideals are found in "The Golden Rule" and in "An Eye for an Eye." Children at early stages of play develop strong feelings about justice. The literature of children is pervaded by stories which teach one or another version of the ideal. The way in which a man comes to view justice will account for much of what he does with his life. He will select his ideal of justice from a wide range of possibilities ranging from, "God helps those who help themselves," to the theologian's ancient cant, "Without hell there can be no justice." Until a man believes something about justice he can not know if he is or is not amply rewarded for what he does; in fact he will not recognize the various forms of being rewarded.

Justice is an abstract noun about which men have little certain knowledge. It has been expressed as an ideal in so many ways that nearly every conceivable human act can be justified. Law attempts to be an approximation of the ideal of justice in the same way a wheel approximates the ideal of a circle, although one might easily suppose the wheel comes much closer to its ideal. Unlike the circle and the wheel, justice and law are constantly changing; and, of course, there is great confusion as to which is which. The American legal system relies so heavily on law that justice very frequently escapes it. Quite probably, the contemporary ideals of justice are better approximated in the informal (and often behind the scenes) operation of the courts than in the formal, open sessions.

Other abstract nouns which stand for ideals are words such as "love," "beauty," "freedom," "courage," "truth," "respect," "pride." Depending on the arrangement one makes in his hierarchy of ideals some of these abstractions will be sovereign, others subordinate, or they may be included in more generalized idealities such as "manhood," "womanhood," "parenthood," "brotherhood." They may also be grouped within idealities of craft or profession as "workmanship," "salesmanship," "scholarship," "statesmanship," and so on. In one way or another, each man must encounter these ideals and come to terms with them. In his language they are abstract nouns, but they are at least as real as the tangible; in fact, they are more real if reality is judged by the criterion of consequences inherent in any of the tangibles of this world.

Ideals are frequently personified or invested in symbols. Personification or symbolization are ancient ways of teaching abstract nouns. American statehood has been personified in George Washington; the ideals of American government are personified in Lincoln. Nearly every organization of charity or service has its ideals symbolized on a plaque or in a banner. The platform balance has been one of several symbols used for justice. Even beyond Christianity, the cross is the symbol of hope or of redemption. If a regiment follows its colors into danger and refuses to suffer their grounding, it is more than a tradition about pieces of cloth. The colors are identified with certain soldierly and manly ideals which are indispensable in a fighting organization.

The symbol is enough. Men who never learn to articulate the meaning of an abstract noun will develop the sentiments, follow the colors, and worship the symbols. Such men will, if anything, be more steadfast and resolute in defense of the symbol than those who understand and articulate the ideal for which the symbol stands. One does not expect to find a nation's most ardent patriots among those who are careful and critical students of its history. In the same respect, the most rigorous students of religion are not apt to be militant adherents to a single creed. This does not imply that it is a good thing to have only critical historians and creedless religionists, or that patriotism and parochialism are bad. A life devoid of sentiment is a poor kind of life. On the other hand, a life of unbridled passion is absurd in a reasonable man. One must seek the Aristotlean mean.[7]

In a word, men must learn to *appreciate* their ideals. Appreciation implies both understanding *and* feeling. When these are joined, tolerance becomes possible. This is one of the long-sought goals of a liberal education and one of the characteristics of a liberally educated man. He can enjoy the sentiments inherent in the symbols of his own religious ideals; derive intellectual satisfaction from his understanding of their meanings; tolerate, in the fullest sense, the idealities of other religions; and derive pleasure from the sentiment and intellectual satisfaction of those who practice them. Appreciation of this kind can only be developed in men by institutions which have a point of view about the nature of the ideal and the numerous ways it is reflected in the affairs of men.

Corruption of the Ideal

There are two ways in which the ideal can excite human feelings; one is in its realization, and the other is in its corruption. There can be no question that the most rewarding feeling one can have about an ideal is through its realization. The regenerating inspiration of the Virgin Mother was described earlier.[8] The living mother is an ever present influence in the plenary ideal of womanhood. To all except literalistic Christians, the influence is allegorical; however, the power it exerts upon the ideal is not diminished because it fails of authentication by the standards of historical realism. The vision of

---

[7] Aristotle, *Nieomachean Ethics Book II*, Parts 4 and 5.
[8] Santayana, *op. cit.*, p. 189.

woman inherent in this symbol has been the theme of countless works of art. Its colloquial vitality merges with other visions and symbols and infuses the whole with benign tenderness and solicitude. Thus conjured is the ideal of womanhood, probably the most civilizing influence in Western man and undoubtedly the most formidable obstacle to his self-degeneracy.

She is the guardian of dignity and the custodian of sentiment whose personal grace in moving and speaking bestows beauty on both object and word. She has a cultivated sense of the arts; her personal relations are constantly tempered in affection, yet she never neglects the edge of her fine animal intuition. Her sexuality is authentic and acknowledged, never subdued and never amplified. She is loyal to mate, devoted to offspring, benevolent to stranger, and bears the anxieties and pain natural to her sex in uncomplaining solitude. She is an ideal, matched in the person of any woman loved by man or child and in the dreams of men and children who have no woman to love. She is an ideal; she is a standard by which men know goodness not only in women but in all things with which she deals, including men.

Properly contemplated, the contemplation of the ideal of womanhood is an experience in beauty. The female form is beautiful; this is a source of beauty which was lost from the Christian expressions of the ideal. By beauty of form is meant the art of Praxiteles and not the adolescent fantasies which decorate the interiors of school lockers or the walls of the barracks. Rather than dwelling on this external and temporal aspect of womanhood, the Christian imagination has concentrated upon the inner qualities which are thought to be eternal. The Christian woman invites her beholders to contemplate her inner radiance which is of the eternal and not of the temporal order. Therefore, exposed or not exposed in its physical representation, the ideal of womanhood is an experience in beauty for those educated to appreciation of the ideal. To those not educated to its appreciation an experience with the ideal of womanhood is absurd, unnatural, and resented.

Those not educated to appreciate the ideal, therefore, delight in its corruption. The ideal of womanhood is discussed here at this length because it appears to be the most widely corrupted ideal in American life. There are both men *and* women who enjoy the burlesque of womanhood. There are women, a few theatrical personalities and nightclub performers, who make of their lives and profession a burlesque of womanhood. The groundlings of today who pack the restaurants which feature nude waitresses (and their counterparts on stage) enjoy the corruption of the ideal of woman because they never came fully to appreciate it. They delude themselves and others that it is the exposure which is enjoyed, but this can be seen any time in numerous expressions far more beautiful. Nor is it their hunger for a shower room scene which brings them in; it is the burlesque of the ideal.

In effect, the observer of the burlesque is a witness of the degradation of a woman. He finds it thereby possible to lay down the burdens imposed by his own manhood and he revels in his animality. It is not correct to say the reveler is totally unaware of the ideal, the simple truth of the matter is that his appreciation of it has not risen to the first level of abstraction. For example, if one were to pass among the predominantly (but by no means exclusively) male audience, pausing with each to make the suggestion that the female performer be replaced by his own mother, daughter, wife, or even a good female friend he admires; the response would not be moderate or gentle.

But the reveler without a capability for abstraction would never understand his own anger at the suggestion. Why would he be offended? In his *Essay on History* Emerson proclaimed, "The creation of a thousand forests is in one acorn."[9] He went on to point out that all of the great civilizations of the world "lie folded already in the first man."[10] In the communion of man, our being flows into us from a single source. Plato might regard this source as the ideal of man. The same source is the ultimate ideal of man and of woman. Thus, in the burlesque of the ideal, the performer is degrading that part of a man's wife, sister, or mother which is woman. The burlesque of womanhood, therefore, diminishes every woman. It is not beautiful; nor is it a beautiful obscenity. It is not just a girl being "naughty." It is usually a shamefully unskilled performer demonstrating that the ideal of womanhood is a sham, a fake, something to be mocked. In a real sense the reveler with even a small capability for abstraction can be brought to recognize that the performer *is* his wife, his mother, *and* his daughter. With such recognition he would, at the very least, take his business elsewhere. In a very short while the consequences

---

[9] Ralph Waldo Emerson, *Essays by Ralph Waldo Emerson* (New York: Thomas Y. Crowell Co., 1926), p. 2.
[10] *Loc. cit.*

of that would bring the performances to an end and do so without the very dubious benefits of raids, arrests, and courtroom pyrotechniques.

It must be re-emphasized that ideals are not chains which hold us in check. Their most important qualities are aesthetic. They appeal to the sense for beauty, and when the aesthetic response begins to warm the imagination, one finds his ideals lead him to a fuller, richer life, a life the human animal can never know. He becomes capable of enlightened justice. He can find, for example, that the literary figure, Lady Chatterly, did not corrupt the ideal of womanhood. He finds her story one which demonstrates the abuses women often suffer at the hands of silly and oppressive institutions. She emerges sympathetically and clothed in dignity despite her encounter in the "four-letter" environment.

Turning to the contemporary arts we are further instructed in the corruption of womanhood by numerous works of fiction which seem to allege that women themselves prefer to be brutalized. "When you go to women," Nietzsche declared, "take your whip with you." This eagerness in philosophy and fiction to debase the nature of women accelerates what appears to be a descent from the ideal. But the animality of female wrestlers is only a curiosity as long as the ideal they corrupt remains alive. If the ideal dies and animality is incarnated as the basic nature of women, who then would care to see such things?

Much of the art of Christians is a vulgarization of Christian symbols. Except for the almost daily improbities it suffers, the ideal of womanhood is no more maligned than the ideal of Christ in the various modern observances of His birth. The commercial Christmas is as much a burlesque of the ideals of Christianity as the offenses against woman burlesque the ideal of womanhood. Often the church has been an unrealizing contributor to the burlesque. Misled into thinking the pseudo-Christian attitudes of seasonal celebrants stem from an authentic sensibility of Christ, the church indulges the material gain, but in so doing it tends to lose ground in its effort to attract the minds and spirits of more reflective men. This effort is the one upon which the fate of the future church hinges.

It now stretches credibility to persuade sensitive and intelligent children that Christmas is a Christian holiday and that all that goes on relates to the birth of a God. Thoughtful Christians are no longer called presumptuous when they suggest, for the sake of their own religion, that Christianity renounce Christmas entirely, accept the pagan origins of a mid-winter feast, and join with all mankind in the enjoyment of a secular holiday. In this way, they can keep the beauty of their religion from the exploiters and corruptors.

Music and drama are foremost among the art forms in suffering from the corruption of the ideals. There appears to be a tendency to corrupt and distort for the sheer joy of corruption and distortion. Occasionally an adventure of this kind becomes not a misadventure but produces a new beauty. But when these felicitious mutations are examined, we find them to have been fashioned by practitioners well schooled and highly skilled in the ideal forms or to have been the work of an authentic genius from whose kindred men have always received new standards of beauty. Aside from these, the rest becomes trash, and there is so much that is trash. But decadence has its own appeal to those who enjoy corruption. So a play which is an organized excuse for obscene gesture and dirty talk will attract much popular attention on the strength of these alone. Those who write it, produce it, and act in it will prosper in every way except artistically; but then, art is not their goal.

We could pass from example to example of how men and women in contemporary life draw pleasure in corrupting ideals. If ideals are influences around which a civilization forms itself and acquires its substance why then are they so capriciously despoiled and degraded? The answer again is in the failure to abstract and to appreciate the ideal. If he is educated to it, a man will be inspired and enriched by his ideals. Any effort to corrupt it will produce his resentment because he has built it into his being. At the same time any aesthetic expression of it awakens one of the enchantments of his life.

Once a child built a house with his building blocks. When it was finished, he sat back and clapped his hands in joy; his appreciation was full. However, his little playmate who had not this appreciation but had the resentment of it knocked the house to the ground. The little one who built the house wept and angered at its loss, and the destroyer knew the joy of destruction. It was a double tragedy. So it is also with the man who does and the man who does not appreciate the ideal. The man uneducated to the beauty of the ideal will not remain indifferent to that which he envies. Such a man, like the resentful playmate, will delight in knocking it down. This, too, is a double tragedy, and the appreciator of the ideal will weep and anger at its loss.

Will we save our ideals? Will we reduce their corruption and distortion? If we will, we will begin by educating children to an appreciation of the ideal.

And this is exactly what we must do.

Teaching the Ideal

How does one teach the abstract noun? A good beginning can be made in that rich and varied lore called children's literature. There is a charming little story called "The Little Red Hen." What is the story about? Virtually every child knows it is about animals that talk with each other; it rounds, rolls, and repeats in that sing-song style in which children delight. The story is about *justice*. Those who work shall eat; those who do not work shall not eat. The wonderland of children's literature is pervaded by abstract nouns. The task of the teacher in mode two knowledge is to develop these nouns into meaningful ideals. Good teachers have always done this; they are doing it now. But a great many teachers pass over the abstract noun, satisfied when the child finds it intelligible by the general standards of reading achievement.

Children's autistic thinking undergoes extension through feats of abstraction. Abstract ideals require thought beyond autistic levels. The humane teacher sees opportunities in reading and in personal relationships. Such a teacher encourages abstraction by moving every figure, metaphor, colloquialism, and relationship against one or another standard of ideality. By such teaching the learner becomes predisposed to value. His hierarchy of ideals is close to his level of consciousness. It is constantly involved in his choosing and he is not a sheep; he is a man. One room supervisor in the Lehigh University Laboratory School develops his classroom climate around the word "respect." "Courtesy," reads a prominent sign, "is respect in action." One can well imagine the hundreds of occasions in the course of a year when the word respect and its role in courtesy must be discussed by the children and teacher of this classroom. In this case the abstract noun is pressed upon the children by a teacher's initiative, and he follows it by constantly insisting that the children interpret its meaning in their daily conduct and relationships with each other. The atmosphere of this classroom is informal; there are no grades; older children help the younger; and through it all children are learning to govern themselves, not by learning rules, but by discovering a single ideal—"respect."

In such teaching the teacher is concerned with what the children can do, and, as it turns out, they can do everything that other children can do. *But he is also concerned with what they are becoming as hu-*

mans. This kind of concern is not found in every classroom, and as the profession's emphasis and the public's anxieties over achievement testing grow, these humane concerns tend to diminish. However, we need not choose either *doing* or *becoming.* With humane classroom teaching there can be both doing and becoming. Every time a P.T.A. or school board is moved to express excessive deference to achievement test scores, the teachers feel called upon to be less concerned for the human development of children. Oddly enough, this sort of thing presently seems to have its greatest harvest in suburban neighborhoods where achievement scores seldom fail to exceed national norms. Beating the norm gives little satisfaction, but beating out a neighboring school is immensely gratifying—losing to it is anathema. Thus, the test item writer is establishing the educational goals for the school and the *becoming* child and his humane teacher have their mandate to perform in the fields of cognate achievement whilst they neglect ideality and feeling.

If there are good things in the court decisions which have banned even the most meager of religious observances from public school, one of those good things may be that theists have been "thrown back on their common humanity." [11] Perhaps they can now, as never before, tolerate the appropriate and tasteful display of the great diversity of religious symbols. Perhaps they can also make visible expression from the great fund of religious art which, like the sign which reads "respect," can be so helpful as *ideal building components* of the school environment. Given the legal and administrative reforms which are needed to assure their unchallenged presence, they should be put into the schools as soon as possible.

A school, if it is anything, is an environment, one which contains as much as possible of the greatness of mankind. Greatness should dominate the environment to the point that it tends to infect all who are part of it. Great teachers are part of it, but it also needs great books, great art, and all manner of things which remind a child of the finest aspects of his human heritage. This need not become a "party line" or a "script." If the school would show Augustine and Anselm, then it would also show Roscellinus and Abelard. If the students would see Locke, show them also Kant. If they would know Hegel, let them also know Whitehead. The school need not take sides between Hamilton or Jefferson in order to have this great American dialectic in their

---

[11] A phrase used by George Bernard Shaw in his appendix to the play, *Pygmalion.*

school environment. Luther and Aquinas are both indispensable spirits in any school which educates its children in humanity.

But, unfortunately, what is true is true. In recent years Americans have been so intent on fashioning "functional" schools which glitter by the roadsides in antiseptic splendor that human greatness has often been omitted. It appears that the imagination of school architects has been afflicted by an overpowering vision of hygienic capsularity. School construction formulae are oppressive enough in numerical form; expressed in art they are grotesque. Yet it is being done every day. Even gone from the walls are the portraits of "the father of the country." In fact, it is possible to enter the bow of more than a few of these streamlined brick, tile, and glass alcazars, travel completely to stern, traversing the midship at several points en route and not encounter a single idea either in personification, symbol, or word during the entire journey.

In developing these educational environments something was forgotten; something important was forgotten. We can say forgotten and not unknown because we once had it; but, like the ancient picture of a second cousin twice removed, when we moved to the new house we left it behind. It is still back there in the one-room school and it would be a good thing for someone to drive by the old schoolhouse one day, pick it up, and bring it to the new building. What is it? It is the abstract noun. Recently this author acquired a pupil desk which was extracted from a one-room schoolhouse. Its framework is an iron casting whose loops weave into a pattern of support for the seat, back and desk. In the middle of this iron work, visible from the side appear the letters of the word "patience."

Down the dusty country road went the American schoolboy of a generation past to enter an environment which was unafraid to extoll the abstract noun. His McGuffey Reader[12] made no bones about its intentions to school him in the virtues of manhood. Even though these virtues are too materialistic for our Twentieth Century values, it serves as an example of value education in a didactical reading program. We may think it a little "corny" to cast them in letters of iron, but if we are to come anywhere near resolving the crisis of values, we must present the abstract noun in some meaningful way, or any hope mankind has for the successful resolution of this unique and difficult crisis will be smothered.

---

[12] Henry Steele Commager, "McGuffey and his Readers," *Saturday Review,* 45 (June 19, 1962), pp. 50-51, 69-70.

So we cannot go on with vocabulary and comprehension as the primary concern of language study. Our ten percent question of a teacher is: "Can they read?" Our ninety percent question is: "What are the human consequences of this reading?" The human consequences of our present language arts education are on view on nearly every newsstand and most bookstores of the city. We have raised up a generation of humans with a technical capacity to read philosophy but with a distinct preference for pornography. These poor, life-starved people, lonely and alone, even though pressed tightly together in transport, street, and domicile must have the trauma of raw sex in their literature, drama, art, and dance because this is the only passion they can know, the only way to convince themselves they are alive.

We must teach our students to pull abstraction from literature. This is the beginning of his capability to idealize and order. The humane teacher must cultivate the reader's feeling for hierarchy and distinction. The power in the literature must become power in the reader as he becomes morticed into a community of great men which is extended vertically through time. Once in communication with this community he can rejoice in its ideals, its vision, its transcendence of materiality and sexuality. He can enter his home library for instant contact with Cicero, Bacon, Milton, Shaw, and James. These are but a few of his personal consultants on manhood who ate bread but did not live by bread alone.

This cry seems one of near desperation! In a way it is, but there is hope. And this voice prefers to be a voice of hope. The task is to bring forth a generation of Americans of which it can be said that each of its members performs the feat of abstraction. Regrettably there are indications that the present corps of professional teachers does not understand this mission as well as some of their professional ancestors. But, hopefully, the challenge has arrived at the very moment we have the instrumentality on hand to do the job. We have the American public school, man's greatest adventure in humanity. Guided properly, this young, vigorous institution, so full of potence and promise, can become the angel of man's destiny. Never before has a single institution shown what can be done for all of the children of all of the people. But it is not enough to know it can be done; we must do it.

So this voice is not one of despair. There is darkness, but the "sun also rises." The schools will rediscover the knowledge and feeling of power. Education students will soon cease their rhapsodizing over cognate knowledge and their empirically based research. They, too, will resume the search for metaphysical meanings in the only place such meaning can exist—in the feelings of men. Men will discover that the word "religion" is broader, much broader, than they had thought, and the movement to higher ground will soon be underway on a general scale. We know this can happen because it is happening. There are teachers who are doing these things now.

A philosopher once asked his student,[13] "Where is the sun?" The young man pointed and said, "Off yonder, there, on the horizon." The sage replied, "You are right and you are not right. The sun is wherever it shines." The light of humane teaching is already shining in many places. It lumens wherever there is a teacher with the vision, the commitment, and the competence to help students to grow in the direction of greatness. Such teachers teach skills, too, but their principal task is making better men. There are many such teachers now, and more are on the way. Soon light will spread to other places where now there is only the darkness of raw measured achievement.

---

[13] Keyser, *op. cit.*, p. 198.

EPILOGUE

A Meditation on the Romance
with Social Science

Men were first charmed by their own imperfections and finally were seduced by them. The seductions occurred in different places and were called by various names. In Vienna it was called psychology and in many other places it was called sociology. These, of course, are not the same things except in their general effects. When men are seduced by their own imperfections they can stand indifferent to that which ennobles.

Alas, this is also the Century of the Third Reich; and, appalled by this and other hideous spectacles of our own time, we have been driven to doubt those great intellectual and artistic endeavors which gave Western man his Renaissance. In the place of this doubt we have installed a sanguine hope that by a science of man we shall root out this depravity which must surely be in our bones. So the three queens embraced new consorts. Philosophy, religion, and education were squired for a time by empiricists, analysts, and clinicians. And men, in this time, have been taught not to feel and not to believe except to feel and believe this new faith called social science.

As in most love affairs, the principal joy lies in expectations. Now those are going and gone, and the realization is growing that we have turned on a helpful new light, but we have not lighted the world, nor are we about to. The queens abashed, bewildered, and a little disappointed will soon resume their dignity and face again the task of humanizing mankind by artistic adventure and metaphysical musing, the only way it has ever been done.

All thought has its origin in feeling, so a thought is merely a shadow of something no other man can know. Those who civilize men must deal first with their feelings and not with the fleeting illusions they call knowledge or events they call experience. What of these consorts now reduced to their life size? There will be recriminations for a time, but this time will pass. It is good occasionally to be carried off into the sunset for an ecstatic night of dreams and blissful hope. But the dawn is here, and we are beginning to see. The romance is over. It is over.

BIBLIOGRAPHY

Aristotle. *Ethics: The Nichomachean Ethics*. Trans.: J. A. K. Thompson. London: Allen and Unwin, 1953.

Beck, Carlton E. *Philosophical Foundations of Guidance*. Englewood Cliffs, N. J.: Prentice-Hall Inc., 1963.

Beck, Robert H. *A Social History of Education*. Englewood Cliffs, N. J.: Prentice-Hall Inc., Foundations of Education Series, 1965.

Beggs, David W. and R. Bruce McQuigg (eds.). *America's Schools and Churches: Partners in Conflict*. Bloomington, Ind.: Indiana University Press, 1965.

Borne, Etienne. *Atheism*. Trans.: S. J. Tester. New York: Hawthorne, 1961.

Brickman, William W. and Stanley Lehrer (eds.). *Religion, Government and Education*. New York Society for the Advancement of Education, 1961.

Buber, Martin. *I and Thou*. Trans.: R. G. Smith. Edinburg: T. and T. Clark, 1937.

Butler, Donald. *Four Philosophies and Their Practice in Religion and Education*. New York: Harper and Brothers, 1951.

Butts, Freeman R. *The American Tradition in Religion and Education*. Boston: The Beacon Press, 1950.

Chaffee, Zechariah, Jr. *The Blessings of Liberty*. Philadelphia: J. B. Lippincott Co., 1956.

Collins, James. *God in Modern Philosophy*. Chicago: Henry Regnery Co., 1959.

Cox, Harvey. *The Secular City: Secularization and Urbanization in Theological Perspective*. New York: The Macmillan Company, 1965.

Descartes, René. *Meditations on First Philosophy* (1641). Trans.: Norman Kemp Smith in *Descartes: Philosophical Writings*. New York: Modern Library, 1958.

Dewey, John. *A Common Faith*. New Haven: Yale University Press, 1934.

Dewey, John. *Democracy and Education*. New York: The MacMillan Company, 1916.

Ehlers, Henry and Gordon C. Lee. *Crucial Issues in Education*. New York: Henry Holt and Co., 1960.

Emerson, Ralph Waldo. *Essays by Ralph Waldo Emerson*. New York: Thomas Y. Crowell Co., 1926.

Flint, Robert. *Anti-Theistic Theories*. London: William Blackwood and Sons, 1879.

Fosdick, Harry Emerson. *A Guide to Understanding the Bible*. New York: Harper and Brothers, 1938.

Gibbon, Edward. *The Decline and Fall of the Roman Empire*. Philadelphia: Claxton, Remsen, and Haffelfinger, 1880, 6 Volumes.

Gibran, Kahil. *The Prophet*. New York: Alfred A. Knopf, 1923.

Guyau, Jean Marie. *The Non-Religion of the Future*. New York: Schocken Books, 1962.

Harthshorne, Charles and William Reese. *Philosophers Speak of God*. Chicago: The University of Chicago Press, 1953; Phoenix Edition, 1963.

Herberg, Will (ed.). *Four Existentialist Theologians*. Garden City: Doubleday, 1958.

James, William. *A Pluralistic Universe*. New York: Longmans, Green and Co., 1909.

James, William. *Essays on Faith and Morals*. New York: Longmans, Green and Co., 1943.

Kallen, Horace. *The Philosophy of William James Drawn from His Own Works*. New York: Modern Library, n.d.

Kaufman, Walter Arnold. *Critique of Religion and Philosophy*. New York: Harper, 1958.

Keyser, Cassius J. *The Human Worth of Rigorous Thinking*. New York: Scripta Mathematica, 1940.

Keyser, Cassius J. *The Rational and the Supernatural: Studies in Thinking*. New York: Scripta Mathematica, 1952.

Kneller, George F. *Introduction to the Philosophy of Education*. New York: John Wiley & Sons, 1964.

Lowrie, Walter. *Kierkegaard*. New York: Harper and Brothers, 1962.

Marty, Martin E. *Varieties of Unbelief*. New York: Holt, Rinehart and Winston, 1964.

Mason, Robert E. *Moral Values and Secular Education*. New York: Columbia University Press, 1950.

Morris, Van Cleve. *Existentialism in Education: What It Means*. New York: Harper and Row, 1966.

Morris, Van Cleve. *Philosophy and the American School*. Boston: Houghton Mifflin Company, 1961.

Nietzsche, Friedrich. *La Gaya Sciencza*. Trans.: Thomas Common as *The Joyful Wisdom*. Edinburg, The Darien Press, 1910.

Pfeffer, Leo. *Church, State, and Freedom*. Boston: The Beacon Press, 1953.

Piaget, Jean. *The Moral Judgment of the Child*. New York: Harcourt, 1932.

Plato. *The Dialogues of Plato*. Trans.: B. Jowett. London: Oxford University 1931 (3rd Edition).

Royce, Josiah. *The Conception of God*. Berkeley: Executive Council of the Philosophical Union of the University of California, 1895; New York: The Macmillan Company, 1898.

Russel, David. *Children's Thinking*. Walthan, Mass.: Blaisdell Publishing Co., Copyright Ginn and Co., 1956.

Santayana, George. *The Sense of Beauty*. New York: Dover Publications, Inc., 1955.

Sartre, Jean Paul. *L'Etre et le neant*. Trans.: Hazel E. Barnes. *Being and Nothingness*. New York: Philosophical Library, 1956.

Smith, T. W. and Marjorie Crene (eds.). *Philosophers Speak for Themselves: From Descartes to Locke*. Chicago: The University of Chicago Press, 1940.

Spinoza, Baruch. *Ethics and De intellectus Emendatione*. Trans.: A. Boyle. London: J. M. Dent and Sons, Ltd., 1913.

Still, Joseph. *Science and Education at the Crossroads*. Washington: Public Affairs Press, 1958.

Tillich, Paul. *The Courage to Be*. New Haven: Yale University Press, 1952.

Weaver, Richard. *Ideas Have Consequences*. Chicago: University of Chicago Press, Phoenix Edition, 1965.

Whitehead, Alfred North. *Religion in the Making*. New York: The Macmillan Company, 1926.

INDEX